LISTEN TO YOUR INNER VOICE

Ellen Hall and James Wawro

vega

To the Inner Voice that speaks to us and to Patricia Jepsen Chuse
who taught us how to listen

Text © Ellen Hall & James Wawro 2001

A catalogue record for this book is available
from the British Library.

ISBN 1-84333-011-3
Printed in Great Britain by
Creative Print and Design Wales, Ebbw Vale

© Vega 2001

A member of the Chrysalis Group plc

First published in 2001 by
Vega
64 Brewery Road
London
N7 9NT
Visit our Website at www.chrysalisbooks.co.uk

We want to hear about your experiences with listening to the inner voice.
Please e-mail us your stories about the inner voice at **www.voicewithin.com**

TABLE OF CONTENTS

Opening this Guidebook

The real voyage of discovery consists not in seeking new lands but seeing with new eyes.

MARCEL PROUST

We used the beautiful June morning to ask our close friends to hike with us in the forest. Six of us, two families with a child apiece, followed the path through the flowering dogwoods. We stepped from stone to stone through the small stream that crossed the trail, getting a little ahead of our friends, who were helping their toddler over the stones. The sound of hooves suddenly punctured the silence. Three men on horses rounded the curve ahead and trotted towards us. We smiled at them. One looked directly back at us with eyes clouded by drugs or drink, grunted and kicked his horse into a gallop. All three horses jumped into action and sprinted through the stream, avoiding the crossing baby only by instinct.

Later that evening, we discussed why we entertain ourselves with mind–dulling diversions, carelessly careening through unhappy lives. From the depths of one hiker's soul came this thought: "Without a connection to the divinity within, there is no peace."

This is a guidebook to that connection within, which we call the inner voice. If we listen to a pang of conscience, a sudden insight, or a creative inspiration, we are learning on our own to explore the largely uncharted territory of our inner world. This book points the way to the major landmarks in the journey of discovery through the unbounded reaches of the human mind. By recounting the experiences of a variety of people (all true and recorded in their own words), we hope to touch a responsive chord in you, our fellow explorer.

We are on a new frontier: we are mapping our inner life. As when explorers of the New World had maps, though incomplete, of the North American continent, assuring them that the new territory was not an illusion–so too, are we just beginning thoroughly to explore the inner world, starting with tantalizingly incomplete texts, both ancient and modern.

The first chapters of this book are the first steps on the inward journey and describe common human brain functions familiar to us all; an understanding of these is essential to reaching the next rungs on the ladder of inner discovery. Intuition, a deep and subtle human brain function, leads us to the discovery that there is an underlying order to the material world, that the order is eminently knowable and that we need only to figure out how to tap into it consistently for a complete understanding of all there is to know on the material plane. Creativity, a yet deeper human brain function, is a process whereby we can use this accessible knowledge to assemble new and better thought forms for our world. Conscience, the first inner "voice" we all recognize, is an inner response determined by a series of subtle, always negative, signals we have absorbed from our culture, guiding us not to take inappropriate action.

At a certain point on this inward journey, the voyage becomes qualitatively different. We are no longer just exploring the brain–we are transcending the material and glimpsing the eternal (Being, All-That-Is, Higher Self, God, or whatever each of us sees as timeless, boundless, fundamental and ultimate). Although we use the same kinds of words to describe our inner map before and after we each reach our unique point of transcendence, there is a different significance to our pursuit once we are in the presence of the eternal; we begin "seeing with new eyes." The transcendent point is each individual's own acknowledgment of his or her own inner voice. As we travel deeper, as we listen more intently with a purer heart, we hear a soundless sound that quietly emanates beauty, truth and goodness into our lives. Our inner voice is eternal, timeless and light-filled: it is love in words.

We will follow the old maps through our investigation of the ancient texts; we will share the inner voice experiences of contemporary explorers, and we will offer some direction to those who wish to follow in their footsteps. The territory awaits your discovery, your breaking through the sound barrier.

So, invite your inner voice. At worst, you could be listening to the highest and best aspects of your own mind–in itself a worthwhile exercise in self-discovery. At best, you could be transcending your individual consciousness and hearing your unity with the universal voice of wisdom–the peak of Self-realization.

> ...as humanity recognizes the Truth... the realm of Spirit will become a new frontier for mankind to explore and master and the last frontier for him as a human being. For in its conquest, he will learn that he is required to master himself first... In its own time, this movement in the human consciousness will dominate all activities of mankind on earth.
>
> THE STILL SMALL VOICE
> BY ROBERT WALL CRARY

CHAPTER I

Hunches, Coincidence and Intuition

Life stories are studded by the mysterious by-products of chance meetings, missed trains, books opening to a significant passage, ajar doors, overheard conversations, a meeting of the eyes across a crowded room.

THE CELESTINE PROPHECY, AN EXPERIENTIAL GUIDE
BY JAMES REDFIELD AND CAROL ADRIENNE

Intuition is awakening to the synchronicity of life. It is glimpsing the great harmony that exists in the universe. When we see a coincidence, we begin to suspect that we are only peeking at an isolated incident in a great synchronized whole. Through intuition we begin to catch sight of the magnificent arrangement of creation. We have the opportunity to acknowledge the unseen world and sense its impact on our lives. Through the seeming chaos of the material world, we begin to see spots of undeniable coordination and harmony. Intuition, that clear, inner knowing that comes without the intellectual effort of gathering the clues, leads us deeper into the uncharted realms of reality.

Getting intuitive glimpses into life's order is like seeing patches of light falling onto the forest floor. We know that a sun-filled sky exists above the forest canopy. We see patches of the reality of the sun, dappling through the trees. Similarly, through the seeming chaos of the material world, we begin to see spots of the undeniable coordination and harmony that exist.

Living intuitively leads us to the celebration of the order in life. An insatiable wonder begins as we realize that even without the arduous task of gathering endless information, all can be known. At first, each time we have an intuitive experience we treasure it in our memory. We think, "Something important just happened, but I am not sure of what it means." Without having painstakingly gathered the evidence, how were we able to know? Our curiosity is piqued. We sense that there must be an unseen order that we have momentarily accessed.

Consider the following experience of

Kevin Peer, a cultural and wildlife documentary filmmaker:

I had worked for National Geographic making wildlife documentaries for several years and was puzzled by the fact that I had never seen a mountain lion in the wild. One day while hiking in Santa Barbara's Guadalupe Dunes County Park I got the sudden urge to follow a deer trail up a ravine. As I made my way along the stream bottom, the going got tough and I was soon sweaty and splattered with mud. After several hundred yards the ravine forked into two narrow tributaries beneath a terrain of high hills and open grassland. I thought that this was a good place to turn around, but a hunch seemed to pull me forward. "Where am I being led to?" I asked silently, and another hunch told me that I needed to turn right and climb out of the ravine.

When I cleared the slope of the ravine and reached level ground, I immediately stopped. I knew this was the place, *right here*, but the place for what? I felt the presence of something behind me and slowly turned around. Sitting there on a patch of bare ground across the ravine from me, eye-level and unmoving, was an enormous mountain lion.

For some reason I was not afraid, even though I knew that if this lion wanted to attack, he could close the distance between us in a matter of seconds—and that I, unarmed and alone, was potential prey. The cat remained in his place, his tail twitching but his face calm, watching me. I slowly sat down and faced him squarely, my eyes slowly engaging his. Minutes passed and we just sat there, watching each other. I knew without a doubt that I had been led here to meet this mountain lion. In one exquisite, fluid motion the lion wheeled around and disappeared into the sage. Had I not followed my hunches, I would never have seen this magnificent animal.

Once we have enough of these intuitive flashes, we can be ready to accept the novel proposition that it is possible to know everything, that at some level all is accessible and we are just catching a glimpse of it, like the light on the forest floor.

Like Alice following the white rabbit in *ALICE'S ADVENTURES IN WONDERLAND*, we begin to pay attention to the strange meanderings of coincidence. We begin to follow the white rabbit where it leads us, ultimately to the Queen of Hearts. We find that it takes active pursuit, patience, and many wrong turns, before we arrive at what we are looking for: the life force, the ultimate honored goal, Being. We find that the best turns are the ones we least expect, and we begin to see the unexpected as a signpost to follow. When we begin to notice coincidence, to ask for clarification, actively to seek help from our intuition, we begin to wake up.

1. Hunches

Everyone has hunches from time to time. As we begin to pay closer attention to our hunches, we learn that we must give up certain patterns to follow those hunches. For example, if we always lunch at a certain restaurant, we have to listen when we "get the idea" to go down the street to another place. Consider the following example:

> On one occasion in 1941, after inspecting anti-aircraft batteries during an actual air raid, Sir Winston Churchill returned to his car. A staff sergeant opened Churchill's customary door, but Churchill hesitated, walked around the car, opened the door on the opposite side of the car and got in, sitting across from his usual position. Driving to their next destination, the

vehicle was struck with the blast of an exploding bomb, directly where Churchill would customarily have been. Said Churchill later: "Something said to me 'stop' before I reached the car door held open for me. It then appeared to me that I was told I was meant to open the door on the other side and get in and sit there—and that's what I did."

2. Coincidence

Consider the following story from Tim Hall, an agricultural consultant, with operations in Jalisco, Mexico:

I have been interested in trees my whole life and have farmed fruit trees commercially. A few years ago I became intrigued with the idea of marketing a fast-growing hardwood that would replace the rainforest trees being so rapidly consumed on our planet. I needed substantial financial backing to go forward in a big enough way to put a dent in the hardwood market.

Flying from Mexico, I boarded a plane that was over-booked. The last seat was in first class, so I was upgraded. I sat next to a prominent, aging businessman, who turned out to be looking for something good to do for the planet with his acquired wealth. He is now financing my first four thousand acres of trees.

This was exciting to me and confirmed to me that there was a greater plan at work and that I was moving toward my destiny in a correct way.

In the popular *Celestine Prophecy*, the first of the nine insights that move the book along is that our spiritual journey is one in which we are led forward by mysterious coincidences. These coincidences have meaning, although sometimes we are not able to decipher exactly what it is.

Some of the twentieth century's leading scientists, including physicists Wolfgang Pauli and David Bohm and neurophysiologist Karl Pribram, have long puzzled over the significance of the coincidences we all find in our lives and the impact that coincidence has on our understanding of the nature of reality. Carl Jung gave serious study to "meaningful coincidences," calling them synchronicity. "Synchronicity suggests that there is an interconnection or unity of causally unrelated events." *COLLECTED WORKS, VOL. 1: PSYCHIATRIC STUDIES.*

3. Being Open to Intuition

> Intuition is the clear conception of the whole at once.
> JOHANN LAVATER

Intuition is the inner knowing that comes without intellectual effort or empirical data to support the knowledge. The thing that we cannot trace is how we arrived at the knowledge. In fact, in order to live intuitively, we have to relax the intellect a bit, direct our attention inward, and listen for what to do or say next.

Intuition requires some turning toward connectedness rather than the chaos of division in the contemporary world. To be open to intuition is to begin to consider that we might all be related to each other and to the earth. If we are all moving to some internal interconnected rhythm, we will meet whom we need to meet; we will find the right store and eat the foods with the proper nutrients; we will follow the right path for us; we will make the contribution we came to make.

Consider how television personality Oprah Winfrey follows her inner feelings rather than her intellect, as described by

Ellen Hall, who met Oprah Winfrey during the writing of this book:

> As a local elected official in Ojai, California, I had the extraordinary experience of meeting Oprah Winfrey during the Spring 1997 filming of her television movie *Before Women Had Wings* on location in our town. I asked her how she went about making her decisions, particularly since she was very successful with risky new ventures, such as her on-the-air book club. Did she pray, go to psychics, listen to advisors, or what? She answered:
>
>> "I live a prayerful life. I'm guided by a desire to do good in the world.
>> The book thing…I don't know…I love books. It was a risky chance I took. I went by an inner feeling…"
>
> I found talking to Oprah like talking with a close friend. She was immediately accessible, personable and sincere. As I watched her on the set, I observed a serious person who understood the impact she had on contemporary culture.

Consider the example of Jack Hart, a teacher of Higher Mind studies:

> One day I was meditating, and an inner voice said: "Buy the stock of Chase Manhattan Bank today". So I did, and then about three months later, it said "Sell the stock of Chase Manhattan Bank next Friday." And so I did. And it had made 40 percent in three months. So it was fine.
> Now, about a year later I was performing an exercise at a workshop, whereby mentally you walked through a forest and came to a clearing, and in the clearing was a little house, and in the house was a wise person, and you went into the house, and you asked the wise person a question. So, I went through this process, and I went in the house and asked the wise person, "What am I supposed to know?" And the voice said: "You're

supposed to know that you're supposed to buy General Electric stock." I said: "Oh, not another one of these things. I don't want to buy General Electric stock if they make nuclear triggers. I'm going to ignore your advice." Well, if I had bought it that day, it went up 100 percent in the next year. I've never had any more stock tips. It's sort of like, "If you're not going to listen to me, then I'm not going to give you any information." So, that's one aspect of the inner voice: it happens a lot more if you listen.

4. Relax the Intellect

In her book PERSONAL POWER THROUGH AWARENESS Sanaya Roman states:

> Your intellect loves to plan everything out in a logical way; your intuition is spontaneous.
>
> * * *
>
> Use your intellect to set goals, to aim you higher. . . . Your intuition will take you there

the best, fastest and easiest way—if you follow your feelings, hunches, inner urges, and deeper desires.

Here's how intuition was accessed by a professional photographer:

> I came up a couple of weeks ago to visit some friends who live on a farm. Their property has a road with an electronic gate and it is a long way to the house. When I arrived, the gate was closed, which I didn't expect. Without the gate code, I would have to drive a half an hour back into town and call for the number. Well, I thought that the last time I had been there that the gate had been a certain four-digit number, and so I entered the number and that wasn't right. They change it every few months.
>
> So, I sat for a moment and I got a figure in my head, but it was my birth date, 1971. So, I said, that can't be right, but I tried it anyway; it

didn't work. The next figure I got, 1965, I entered it in and it was the right one. The gate opened.

5. Have Faith That There Is a Plan

Intuition supposes that somewhere all is known or that there is a blueprint to be tapped into where the whole picture is available, beyond the limited perspective of our own personal consciousness.

Consider this example, from Robby Romero, an Apache living in Taos, New Mexico, and a musical artist:

> During a visit to Japan in the early 1990s to promote the Sacred Run and to play my music, I befriended a Buddhist monk who one day asked me to assist him in establishing a Peace Pagoda on Roosevelt Island in Manhattan across from the United Nations. At the agreed-upon time we flew to New York, were picked up at the airport by Buddhist monks living in New York and drove to Greenwich Village to have dinner at a Japanese restaurant owned by a friend of the monks. Because we were planning an extended stay, most of our worldly belongings were in the trunk of the car. During dinner, we got to know the owner of the restaurant and generally had a good time.
>
> After dinner, we returned to the car to find that the trunk had been broken into and everything in it stolen—guitars, clothes, even extra pairs of shoes. We went to our hotel to figure out what to do, but it quickly became clear that our worldly goods were gone. At about 4:00 a.m. we received a call from the owner of the restaurant saying that he had been approached by one of the street people to purchase various items, including a leather bag with fringe and bead work on it. Feeling somehow that I should have these items, he bought the bundle and was calling to ask me to come down to look at it.

Needless to say, I was overjoyed: the bag was my medicine bundle (the thieves had not even opened it) containing all of my sacred objects, including my ceremonial "chanupa" (or pipe) which I had fashioned by hand during ceremonies from a single block of stone. The restaurant owner's intuition had rescued something very dear to me. I thought for a long time over the fact that the only one of my worldly possessions that had returned to me (in New York City, of all places) was that which was sacred.

Intuition is the breaking through of your understanding that there is a whole program out there that is available for you to know without the intellect. It is a way of knowing that far surpasses our mind's traditional learning. Follow your intuition and it will become strengthened even as it becomes more subtle.

Virginia Sky, a choreographer from Sierra Madre, California, had the following experience:

I was living in a cottage surrounded by flowers over on Aliso Street. The guy next door was a biker and seldom at home. He was not taking care of his dogs, which just was driving me crazy because I love animals. He had two dogs, and they fought. The two of them somehow got together one day and they were going to rip each other out. I don't know where I got the strength because they were both big animals—not Great Danes, but a cross between a Great Dane and a German Shepherd. These were big animals. When I heard the dogs fighting, I went over and pulled the smaller dog off, took him in the house, and helped all of his wounds. I was totally exhausted, he was panting. I chained the other dog up. They didn't hurt me; both dogs liked me.

Right when I was helping this dog, this calm came over me like—"you're supposed to help, you're supposed to help."

Then, I took the dog to the vet, and I had $50 left to do Christmas presents for my family in Cleveland. That's what the vet bill was, $50. I paid it and I came home, and I thought, "What am I going to take back to Cleveland?" I had a dream that night about a blue light (I've been told that when an angel is around you, they come in the form of a blue light), and that blue light just hovered around me and it just—like they thanked me.

The next day, there was a knock at the door, it was the UPS man. He gave me this package that was rolled up, and I thought "I didn't order anything." It turned out to be from a woman, a family friend, I had asked a year ago to sketch a picture of the house I grew up in in Cleveland. She not only sketched it, she gave me three different pictures with three different types of paint, so I gave those as my

Christmas gifts. She wrote: "I don't want to charge you for these." So, there was the $50 that I was going to pay for Christmas gifts. The whole event was just this very natural exchange. So, sometimes I just think we're doing right what we're supposed to be doing.

6. Follow Your Intuition

When you have an intuitive experience, follow through. Test it. An example:

I had a great friend who lived on the East Coast so we saw each other irregularly. I kept getting the feeling to call her, but then my mind said, "but I have nothing to say and it's so expensive, I'll do it later." Unknown to me she had Lyme disease and died within the month. We were only able to talk for a few minutes before her passing. Why had I not listened to this intuition?

With intuition you don't get the whole future, just one step at a time. I only got the intuition to call her, not the information that she was ill.

Sometimes, intuition is so strong that it seems to speak to us as an outer voice. Consider the following example:

I was in the Sespe Wilderness in the Los Padres National Forest. It was warm, and we were on a hill, and I wanted to stop for awhile and enjoy a cool breeze. I lay down on the trail, because everything else was kind of scrubby, and I just started dozing off. This wonderful—you know how just going off to sleep sometimes can just be really beautiful, and I heard this voice say "Ellen, get up!" It was so strong, it was like—I looked around to see who it was. I got up. I just popped me right up straight. Then, I was going down the trail, and I turned around and there was a rattlesnake coming down the trail. Just coming right at me, you know, without any sense that I was there, and I had been asleep, basically.

Does following our intuition compromise our free will? Of course, we are free not to follow intuition. When we do follow our intuition, we have freedom from danger, accidents, confusion. We become free to meet compatible situations and people, to be at the right place at the right time, to be of service, to have the perfect thing happen to us rather than second best. Life can be challenging, but it need not be hard.

7. Results

Oh, the difficulty of fixing the attention
of men on the world within them!

SAMUEL TAYLOR COLERIDGE

The result of living intuitively is increased harmony. We call our sick friends when they need to hear from us. We avoid situations with rattlesnakes.

Often when we need to call people or ask them a question, we'll run into that person at the post office, or they will call on another matter. When we operate from intuition, things happen easily; and, as our intuitive abilities increase, the coincidences increase.

Consider the following example from an advertising professional:

> I ask my higher self about the most mundane things and the most profound things. I'll ask, sometimes, about certain foods. People tend to get really connected to food in a desirous fashion, like abundance and deprivation are connected to food. So, rather than letting that be what leads me to food, I'll say: "Okay, what do I need today, or do I need this, or do I need that?" I'll get real strong senses of it. Food is a great one to do it with also because, when you're on the right path and you're eating the right thing, everything else is also right—an inner peace can also happen with that. It's an interesting thing, because it's like a communing with your body and your soul.

In her book *LIVING IN THE LIGHT*, Shakti Gawain uses the analogy of the conductor. Each of us plays a unique instrument conducted by a universal intelligence. If we play our part without regard to the conductor's direction or the rest of the orchestra, we have total chaos. Intuition is following the conductor, and its consequence is harmony.

Consider the following example of Patricia Jepsen Chuse, a spiritual teacher in Tucson, Arizona:

> We've been out of balance on the planet, as human beings. When we can begin to become aware and focus on our intuition and allow it to operate through us, and agree with it, and respect it, then we begin to shape up

and bring ourselves back into balance and alignment with our universe. We are not separate, going our separate ways. We're absolutely complementary to everything else, including all of nature. I think the inner voice does not just concern me or you. I think it's an impersonal creator and impersonal guide. It is of infinite intelligence that guides everything. So, when it's guiding me to move in some direction, it's also taking into consideration where the snake is, where the squirrel is, and where the mountain lion is.

Another result of intuitive living is less stress and increased vitality. Without accidents, missed planes, struggle and conflict, we are more calm. We are also more assured that if we can get in step with the cosmic universe, everything will go smoothly, what we need will appear when we need it. When you are successful at increasing your intuitive response to life, you essentially relax. When you are less focused on making things happen, and more focused on letting them happen, you feel more excitement about life, more health and more peace (although it is mixed with the uncertainty of not knowing what will happen next). This way of living may be described as an exciting peace.

> There is nothing pleasurable except what is in harmony with the utmost depths of our divine nature.
> HEINRICH SUSO

HOW TO

Intuition

A New York City business executive:

Many of my friends are on diets of various types, but I recommend to them a very simple one: five minutes before you go to lunch, or eat anything, get quiet for a moment (even go to the washroom if need be) and ask your body "What do you need for nourishment at this time?" Regardless of whether the answer is chocolate cake or chicken sandwich, follow it! You will be amazed at the results.

TRY IT!

Perhaps you've been on a diet and found it hard to decide what to eat at any particular meal. Try using your intuition to provide answers as the New York businessman suggests.

- Take five minutes before you go out to lunch and sit straight in a quiet, comfortable place.
- Take a few deep breaths until you are relaxed.
- State the question by mentally asking your body: "What do you need for this meal?"
- Wait and listen. Don't be discouraged if an immediate answer doesn't come at first–you may get it on the way to the restaurant or when the menu is open before you.
- When the answer does come, follow your intuition.
- See how the selection makes your body feel.

TRY IT!

A councilwoman:

When I need to shop for clothes, I decide what the look is
I'm going after and ask where to go. I try to get an
impression of which store my intuition is leading me to.
I usually get a picture of the store in my mind. I have to
give up the idea of how much money I want to spend
(but spending the money has always turned out okay
anyway). Often I get the picture in my mind of the outfit
itself–I'll see a pair of jeans or a light-colored suit. When
I get to the store, I look for the jeans rack or the light
suits. It's always there. I save a lot of time wandering
from store to store and department to department.

√

TRY IT!

Shopping can be fun–but it can also be a horrendous waste of time. You can use your intuition in the following manner to make shopping more efficient:

- When you find yourself needing to buy something, stop for a moment in your home.
- Sit in a quiet, comfortable place; take a few deep breaths until you are relaxed.
- Ask "Where do I find the article that I am looking for?"
- Listen for the stores that come to mind and follow the answers you get.
- If you do not receive an immediate answer, forget about it, and see how often what you need seems to pop up in front of you as your intuition leads you to what you asked for.

CHAPTER II

Creativity

The Artist's Way is a spiritual journey home to the self…. What I call my marching orders others may sense in themselves as a still, small voice or, even more simply, a hunch. The point is that you will hear something if you listen for it. Keep your soul cocked for guidance.

THE ARTIST'S WAY
BY JULIA CAMERON

Creative living includes an aspect of the inner voice we have been discussing: reliance on inspiration that can come only from within. As with any other intuitive experience, it requires us to pay close attention to what we "hear" our inner voice saying.

But something sets creativity apart from the rest of intuitive brain function. Inspiration is only part of creativity. In order to create something, a procedure must be followed; and an easily identifiable four-step creative process becomes evident after reading the accounts of the many great artists, scientists and musicians who have experienced creativity. They all tell similar stories of HOW they create. For example, Wolfgang Amadeus Mozart wrote the following in a letter to a friend (from THE LIFE OF MOZART, by Ernest Holmes):

When I am, as it were, completely myself, entirely alone, and of good cheer... it is on such occasions that my ideas flow best and most abundantly. Those ideas that please me I retain in memory and ... it soon occurs to me how I may turn [them] ... to the various peculiarities of the instruments. All this fires my soul, and ... the whole, though it be long, stands almost complete and finished in my mind. ... I hear them, as it were, all at once. What a delight this is I cannot tell! ... When I proceed to write down my ideas ... the committing to paper is done quickly enough, for everything is, as I have said, already finished ....

Consider the following example of Walter T. Haswell, a metallurgical engineer from Syracuse, New York, :

I know that when it comes to creativity on a new scientific principle, or a new invention, you have to go in and learn everything that can be learned on the subject. Then, you forget it all, just turn it over to Spirit. Suddenly, "Eureka," there's the whole thing laid out for you, here's how this should be done. That's how creating new technology works for me. But, I've never been able to do that without the intensity of the background preparation.

1. Step One: Research

Immersion in the subject you are interested in is the fundamental building block to creativity. This is a time when you will want to study everything you can get your hands on about the subject. Your interest and enthusiasm push you forward. The step of research is necessary because it is your responsibility to assemble the building blocks at your command for creation. It is like Mozart creating a beautiful piece of music: he first needed the ability to play the piano and write music, before the music came to him.

Consider Jim's experience in the following situation:

> An American Bar Association sub-committee was given the task of finding a solution to a serious problem in international law: how to develop a statute which would voluntarily, but effectively, prevent inconsistent judgments in a world where every nation with any jurisdictional contact with an international commercial dispute has the power to issue a judgment binding the disputing parties. We studied the problem off and on for over a year. We had the brightest minds in the field of international commercial disputes on the subcommittee. We researched the law of most civilized jurisdictions to find precedent, but we came up empty-handed.

We identified all of the pieces to the puzzle, and ultimately concluded that no more research would be useful—either the problem could be solved with what we knew from our laborious research, or there was no solution.

One morning while jogging with my mind wandering, I realized that I knew the answer to the problem. The awareness was like being stopped at a red light, looking away from the traffic signal, looking back at the signal and realizing that the light was green and that you could go forward. The solution was elegantly simple and later became the Conflicts of Jurisdiction Model Act. We could never have even understood the problem without thoroughly studying the options, the precedents, the issues and the ways other efforts had failed; and we could never have gotten the solution at all without inspiration from the inner voice.

2. Step Two: Forget It

Patience and the creative process are directly related.　　　　PATRICIA JEPSEN CHUSE,

TEACHER OF HIGHER MIND SUBJECTS

Often quite abruptly you feel saturated with the subject. Your interest wanes. You drop your study, and all you want to do is go to the beach or listen to jazz or take a hike. If you understand the creative process, you accept this stage and relax into it. It is that time in the creative process when your being demands time quietly to calculate and assemble the building blocks that you have placed there for the intuitive inspiration. The length of the gestation period is not up to the human creator—some creative inspirations have not happened until years after the assembly of the building blocks.

When the Chrysler Corporation realized the need for a new vehicle to capture the imagination of its customers, it put intensive study into what consumers wanted. Thereafter, many planning meetings were held to synthesize the results of the studies and decide upon a new automobile. At some point, the story goes, Lee Iacocca stopped attending all planning meetings and instead went about his other business and began attending symphonies in his spare time. During one of the symphonic performances, he got the idea for the 1983 Chrysler Mini-Van.

This is a difficult step for workaholics or even hard workers, to give themselves permission to play. When we have pretty much amassed the database of information needed to solve the problem, we must then give up control and get in the hammock.

That's when creativity happens.

Maia Aprahamian, composer, on "walking away," quoted in *WISDOM AND THE SENSES: THE WAY OF CREATIVITY*, BY JOAN M. ERICKSON (1988):

> At some point, the work does take on its own life, and one has to let go of control to a certain degree, and become partners with it.
>
> But at this point also, there can come a dry place—the proverbial desert where no idea is right, and nothing seems to work. I have found it takes a combination of futile struggling, and just walking away from it. One without the other doesn't work, but I have no idea why. It's often tempting to quit, or just put it aside and never get back to it. But eventually "the desert shall blossom the rose," and one never knows when that rainfall will come.

3. Step Three: Ah-Ha!

I did not search; I found.

PABLO PICASSO

Eureka! ["I have found"]

ATTRIBUTED TO ARCHIMEDES,

So often does inspiration come when we least expect it that it is not unusual for creative persons to actually exclaim or shout when they realize that the answer to their search has come. They say it: "Ah-Ha." Inspiration comes as a quick mental picture or as a fully formed thought. It may come while we are in the shower, or exercising or commuting to work, or at any other time when our intellect is not strongly focused on any particular set of thoughts. We may become aware of the inspiration like a flower in our hand, and often it appears to be outside of the logical process. It is discovered rather than constructed. It is as if the searchlight of our mental powers sweeps over the field of our brain and lights the fully formed inspiration it falls upon.

A. Accessing Inspiration

Inspiration can be accessed in a variety of ways. Napoleon Hill, in *THINK AND GROW RICH*, described a method used by Dr. Elmer Gates of presenting oneself for inspiration, or, as Dr. Gates himself put it, practicing "the art of mind-using." Dr. Gates was the originator of over 300 patented ideas, using a method he called "sitting for ideas."

Dr. Gates set up a "personal communication room" which was insulated from outside noise and light. He furnished it with a table and a pad of paper. In this dark, quiet room, Dr. Gates would go over the known facts about his current invention project until ideas flashed in his mind.

Writing for hours at a time, he brought to light many new inventions. He was also paid to "sit for ideas" by some of the most successful American corporations of his day.

Older cultures devised ways to access creative ideas. In eighteenth-century Ireland, a prestigious school for poets used the following method (from *THE ENCYCLOPEDIA OF CELTIC WISDOM*, by Caitlin and John Matthews):

> I must not omit to relate their [the poets'] way of study, which is very singular. They shut their doors and windows for a day's time and lie on their backs, with a stone upon their belly and plaids about their heads, and their eyes being covered, they pump their brains for rhetorical encomium or panegyric: and indeed they furnish such a style from this dark cell as

is understood by a very few.

... Marquis of Clanricarde in his **Memoirs Of 1722** ... describes visiting a poetic school. It was open only to descendants of poets and was situated well away from disturbances of any kind. The House of Memory was a low hut, with no windows to let in the day nor any light at all used but that of candles. The professors gave a subject suitable to the capacity of each class ... the said subject having been given overnight, they word it apart each by himself upon his own bed, the whole next day in the dark, 'til a certain hour in the night, lights were brought in, they committed it to writing. Each student then dressed and gave a performance of his work to his teacher, and was given a fresh subject to study in the dark.

We each experience creativity in different ways. Isolation is not the way for everyone to access inspiration. It has been said about one famous sculptor that he struggled for years to make enough money from his work to be able to move out of his storefront studio in a rowdy section of a large American city. Finally, he scraped together enough to move to a pastoral setting 75 miles north of the city. For the next year, he appreciated natural beauty, drank wine, ate pasta, and got fat, but he created nothing. It was only when he got the old storefront location back that he began to sculpt again.

Similarly, this California filmmaker is inspired by being around creative people and their creations:

> I tend to need stimulus when I'm looking for creativity. A lot of times, I just carry around tons of ideas and it never stops, I'm constantly being drilled by my own inspirations. But, I do get very, very motivated and inspired by other people's works of art. So, when I want to be really creative, I tend to go out and buy magazines, or books, or go look at art, and it will immediately thrust me into, like the heart of creativity. Whereas, if I try to go and just be alone, at a desk or something, it's very difficult for me to be creative.
>
> I get a sense when I am heavily in the creative zone. I feel this incredible energy where I'll wake up at 6:00 in the morning, just with my whole body vibrating. It's the weirdest feeling, and I have to get up and I have to do something. I'm always, in some way, in the creative zone, but there are times when I'm really working, where it just multiplies and it keeps going. I think in a continuous consciousness about creativity or work, like working on a lot of different projects keeps it going. It's like watering the garden, it just keeps growing. So, for me, the best thing to do is to always have something going on, some kind of project.

B. Capturing Inspiration

What is the role of the human creator in all of this? Throughout history great writers have invoked the "Muse" which may be nothing more than access to creativity. For example, <u>Homer began his epic poem *THE ODYSSEY* with the words "Speak to me Muse about a noble and worthy man.</u>" It is the role of the creator, or the artist, to capture as much of the complete idea as possible when the Muse is operating, or the inspiration is coming through. It is the expression of the inspired idea that manifests the creation, and the greatest artists manifest the creation most faithfully to the original inspiration.

C. The Source of Inspiration

The question arises: where do these creative inspirations come from? Here are comments of famous creators:

Leonardo da Vinci said: "Where the Spirit does not work with the hand there is no art."

On nearly every piece of music composed by Johann Sebastian Bach was written: "To God alone, the glory."

Frederick Heart, a professional sculptor, said: "<u>Creativity is being receptive and allowing the work of God to reverberate on you, to reflect on you.</u> You are composing your reactions and reflections. There is only One Creator."

Billy Joel, in describing the creation of his song "The River of Dreams," recounts that he first heard the song in a dream and that the song he heard was much better than the song he finally wrote. As soon as he became aware in his dream that he was hearing a new song, he awoke and wrote down as much of the completed thought as he could. The energy of the vision carried through to the writing of the song, and the success of the song depended upon how faithfully he was able to capture what was given to him.

4. Step Four: Manifestation

Our logical, practical, reality-based being takes over in this last step. We are required to be disciplined–but manifesting, or bringing our inspiration into physical reality, is an essential element of all creation. Why is it that we were given the inspiration if not to help it blossom into reality? The more we understand that manifesting is our responsibility in the creative process, the more creative inspiration we are given. Discipline is necessary to carry into reality what has until that point been only a vision. However, the vision carries with it the energy to open up all the doors and remove all the blocks to the final rendering into reality of the vision.

For example, when we got the idea for this book, we talked about the general subject of the inner voice and about the fact that a book logically stepping through the phases of the inner voice had never been written. We decided to do it. We collected our sources and researched the subject. Now it was time to write, but where were we to begin? After quieting the mind and asking for the organizing principles for this book, we found that the titles to the seven chapters came. The process took only a few seconds yet produced a road map that has stood the test of time. We developed the outline, conceived of the subchapters, completed our research, interviewed each of our subjects, talked about all of the concepts, and actually wrote every word of the book–a necessary exercise in the manifestation of the book you are holding.

> *CREATIVITY'S FOUR STEPS:*
> - *Research*
> - *Forget it*
> - *Ah-ha*
> - *Manifestation*

5. What Creativity Is Not

In determining what creativity is, it is useful to demonstrate what creativity is not. It is not just splashing paint on the canvas or sitting down with the pen poised over blank paper, drawing circles and hoping that words will come out. It is not a frenzy of spontaneity and abandon. It is not turning on the music and swirling around with a colored scarf. If we want to create a dance, for example, we must first study how the body moves and how these movements express feelings and attitudes. Studying and training give us the necessary tools with which to express our creations. No great composer just sits down and bangs out a new piano concerto without ever having learned how to play the piano. Einstein did not create the theory of relativity without studying physics.

On the other hand . . .

Have you ever heard of a musician who is technically perfect, but has no creativity? There are artists who can paint perfect copies of the masters but never create their own, original works. These people have obviously studied and have the tools they need. Why aren't they creative? How many competent physicists have never come up with a new theory? The answers lie in the concept of "balance."

6. Balancing the Right and Left Brain

I would go without shirts or shoes,
Friends, tobacco or bread
Sooner than for an instant lose
Either side of my head.

KIM

BY RUDYARD KIPLING

We have two hemispheres in our brain. Each side has distinct functions. The left hemisphere is involved with language and analysis of stimuli in terms of details. The right hemisphere seems to be more involved with spatial tasks, such as picturing the floor plan of a house or recognizing a face. The right hemisphere also deals with our emotions, timelessness and dreams.

The creative process uses both sides of the brain in a balanced way. Consider creativity's four steps: (1) Research, (2) forget it, (3) Ah-Ha! and (4) Manifestation.

Number 1, Research, is a detail- and language-oriented task. Numbers 2 and 3, Forget it and Ah-Ha!–relaxing and being receptive to inspiration–are both more dreamy, right-hemisphere processes. Number 4, Manifestation, requires logical, organizational and time-sequencing procedures, which are more left-hemisphere. So, we have two creativity steps in the right hemisphere and two steps in the left, a process requiring a balance of both hemispheres. If we function in this balance of capabilities, our lives will blossom with creativity. Our challenges will be handled graciously. We will find ourselves in the right livelihood, and it will use a perfect blend of our left-brain talents and our right-brain inspiration from within.

The steps in the creative process are frequently not logical, yet the completed creation can have the simple elegance of impeccable logic. In order to compose a symphony, you must understand the fundamental rules of music so that you can combine these tools into a pattern that is beautiful. You must relax from the effort when you feel the need. You must capture the inspiration when it flows. And you must do the work of publishing the music for the world to hear.

Creativity is capturing the beauty, truth and goodness of the eternal realities. These realities comprise everything there is, the abandon and the discipline.

7. Living a Creative Life

He not busy being born is busy dying.

BOB DYLAN, "It's Alright, Ma"

The creative process applies not just to art, but to living a creative life. If we live today exactly the way we did yesterday, we are not Being. But if we take a fresh look at each life situation, we begin to live creatively. And that is the job of all of us who are not principally painters or musicians: how to incorporate creativity into our daily lives.

Michael Toms, a radio program producer in Ukiah, California, puts it this way:

> I think everybody is here to be creative and creativity is intimately connected with the soul and the deeper self. And as we open the channel to our deeper self and our own soul life, creativity will only be enhanced and expanded. So absolutely [creativity] is connected [to the inner voice].
>
> Personally, I find it important to spend more time being than doing. . . not exactly more time, but have a balance in your life of being and doing. If your doing comes from being, you're going to be okay. Creativity is manifestation. If your being comes out of doing, then it's much more problematical. We live in a *do, have, be* society, like if you *do*

this, you can *have* that, then you can *be*. I'm suggesting that it should be a *be* instead of a *do* where the doing comes out of the beingness and then you have whatever you have. We have it reversed from the way it's supposed to be, and if we can turn it around, and actually get into our beingness and allow that to unfold, rather than simply doing....
If you think of a great artist, a great painter, a great writer, a great whoever, anybody who is creative in whatever they are doing, they usually have an obvious beingness. It's unique to them and it's obvious they are doing something that's coming out of their inner soul, their inner guidance and inner self. It's like you can't do anything else but that when you're in touch with that energy.

Consider the following guidance received by a Minnesota spiritual advisor:

When I was asked to conduct a seminar at a retreat for priests, all male, I was concerned about being a woman preaching to priests. In doing some soul-searching about what to say, I got the inspiration to use as my course the questions asked by God or Jehovah in the Old Testament and by Christ in the New Testament. The seminar was a great success, the pertinent questions were thought-provoking and profound, and gender was taken completely out of the equation.

HOW TO
Creativity

We are all creative. You are too. Think about your own job. It is not automatic; different situations arise requiring your thought and different application of your skills. But don't you usually solve the challenges that arise in your work, even if you cannot precisely say initially what the solutions might be? If you do not think you are creative, catalogue the times during the past month when you could not solve the challenges presented in your job. Now catalogue the times during the past month when you did solve the challenges. Compare the two numbers. Are you creative?

DO IT!

Serena wanted a special party for her thirteenth birthday. She made a list of her girlfriends and talked to her mother about a budget. Then she puzzled over what kind of party would be the most fun for her and her friends. She looked at teen magazines, went to party supply stores and talked to everyone about good theme parties they had been to. She seemed to have forgotten about the party when one afternoon she suddenly bolted out of her room with a luau on her mind. The girls were invited to wear Hawaiian clothes; leis were used as party favors; the guests danced the hula together; the birthday cake was pineapple cake; and her thirteenth birthday party was a great a success.

TRY IT!

- To test your creativity, give a party for your friends. Begin assembling your thoughts about who should attend, when it will be, how long it will take, where it will be held, and what it will cost.
- Quiet your mind for a moment and ask whether the party could have a theme; ask what the menu could be; ask what entertainment would liven up the party.
- If your enthusiasm seems to fade, forget about it for awhile and wait for inspiration.
- When the inspiration comes, write it down.

DO IT!

Richard decided that he wanted to re-landscape the back-yard. Driving around the neighborhood, he started notic-ing yards and realized that a patio cover could be a great addition. He looked at some books from the library about patio cover designs. He put up on the refrigerator a picture of a patio cover design he liked from the Sunday newspa-per. In surveying the backyard, Richard found some unex-pectedly useful things, like big, beautiful boulders that had been covered with leaves. After a few days of thinking about the design, he felt indifferent to pursuing any more information about backyard designs. Sitting at dinner looking out the back window one night, he got the idea to move the boulders and to create a pond. He drew a rough picture of how he saw the backyard. Then he drove to the hardware store and got the materials to build the patio cover. After building the patio cover, he figured out how to install the pond using the boulders, and planted flowers and bushes.

TRY IT!

Here are the steps:

- Pick a project and gather the information about it.
- Give the ideas time to germinate in your mind.
- When any ideas come, write them down. As you are writing, fill in any other ideas that come.
- When the plan is finished, complete the project.

CHAPTER III
Conscience

1. The Inner Voice with a Message

The inner knowings we have been discussing usually come to us as a feeling or a thought, and they come with no moral content. The one inner voice we all recognize is conscience, which often does come as a "voice," and which always has a moral message.

2. Childhood–Conscience Awakens

> Let your conscience be your guide.
>
> JIMINY CRICKET

The voice of conscience may be the first inner voice that we hear. Like Jiminy Cricket in the Walt Disney version of *Pinocchio,* our conscience sits on our shoulder and says: "No." It told Pinocchio not to play with the bad boys but to go straight home from school.

When do we first experience conscience? Research shows that this occurs at the "age of reason," when we make our first moral judgment, at about six years of age.

Does conscience come from within the child, or is it learned from parents and environment? We all have a conscience. We all have heard our conscience "speak" to us. Have we ever stopped and asked ourselves: "What is that conscience? Where does it come from? What 'sound' does it make? Why is it there?" When we stop to ask such questions, we begin to see the first glimmerings of the grand scheme of the universe. We begin to hear the first faint sounds of an inner voice.

First, what is conscience? Certainly, it is a familiar voice. We hear it say, "stop gossiping," just as we are getting into a delicious story that could put a friend in a compromising light.

Conscience is inner advice about a moral choice, an internal knowing of "right" from "wrong."

What does it sound like? We all have a continuous, soundless inner monologue chattering away in our minds: "will the green one clash with the blue one?" "the baby is cute," "the car needs a service." The "voice" of the monologue is so well known to us–we have been hearing it since we were young–that it seems simply an inherent component of our lives. Occasionally, however, that voice will take on a more forceful quality: "Don't do that!" This more forceful direction of our own internal voice about a moral choice, we call conscience. All people have this experience. In fact, this soundless voice is so universal that, if for some reason we don't have it, and are thereby unable to perceive our social and moral obligations, society calls us psychopathic!

Why do we experience this soundless internal voice in moral choices? Where does it come from? Is conscience a reaction learned from our environment, or is it an internal direction from some higher power? Robert Coles, in his book *THE MORAL INTELLIGENCE OF CHILDREN*, concludes:

> We grow morally as a consequence of learning how to be with others, how to behave in this world, a learning prompted by taking to heart what we have seen and heard. The child is a witness; the child is an ever-attentive witness of grown-up morality–or lack thereof; the child looks and looks for cues as to how one ought to behave, and finds them galore as we parents and teachers go about our lives, making choices, addressing people, showing

in action our rock-bottom assumptions, desires and values, and thereby telling those young observers much more than we may realize.

Is conscience just a psychological function? Is it simply a gathering of "do"s and "don't"s we acquire through the subtle influence of parental attitudes and directives? Do our psyches log in rewards and punishments, then compute and program a conscience response? Or does our conscience reflect more subtle influences around us?

Culture has been cited as the author of conscience. Isn't conscience the foundation of social order? What else keeps citizens from taking what does not belong to them, hurting their fellows, unleashing unkindness and generally frustrating the social compact?

The voice of "No!" is a seemingly fundamental sense, like seeing color.

When George Washington, as a schoolboy, wrote: "Strive to keep alive in your breast that little spark of celestial fire–*conscience*," he expressed the widely held view that conscience is spiritual. However, as we will see, conscience is just our internal note of "no," and the belief in conscience as spiritual may be related to the belief in a punishing God.

3. Right and Wrong

The beginning of all ethical inquiry has been to separate "right" from "wrong." But how do we know what is "right"? Where does such "knowing" come from and why do we follow it? Is conscience God's "still small voice within," referred to in the Bible (I Kings 19:12). Or is conscience an alternating blend of individual moral intuition and all of the judgments we have learned from experience and from our society?

> ... there is nothing either good or bad, but thinking makes it so....
>
> — HAMLET, ACT 2, SCENE 2

4. A Separate Voice

Conscience is understood by each of us in different ways. To some, it is an internal guidance system taking us to what we want; to others, it is social right or wrong; to many it is the voice of heaven. But in everyone's common experience, it is a separate voice, different in authority, if not tone, from the internal voice we hear in every waking moment.

Consider the concept of conscience as expressed by a Hollywood film director:

No, I don't see conscience as being the same thing as the inner voice. Conscience, I think, is much more environmental. I think it's connected to shame and guilt, the way we grow up perceiving right and wrong. Conscience can apply to so many different things. It's everything from sex, to money, to friendships. Everything we do socially is touched with a certain amount of conscience, but that has to do with shame and guilt. I think that's very different from truth. It's much more about viewpoints. As children, we grow up and we hear a lot of other people's viewpoints. You almost can't help but take everyone else's viewpoints on. As you grow older, you have to use your inner voice to then separate out everyone else's viewpoints from your own knowingness.

Consider also the following concept of conscience held by Neale Donald

Walsch, author of *CONVERSATIONS WITH GOD*:

What we have, rather than conscience, is really an internal guidance system. It's a little beacon inside of us that tells us how to get to where we want to go, and how to be who we truly want to be, and that has nothing to do with right and wrong; it has to do with our conceptualization of self, of who we are.

That's why certain people can do things that you and I would call wrong, and do them with impunity. It doesn't seem wrong to them. Indeed, in their own inner guidance system, it's not wrong. It's precisely what they need to do in order to be who they really are. Which explains the phenomenon of Adolf Hitler, or Idi Amin, or any of those strange, extraordinary people who have dotted the landscape of human history and who have made

decisions and undertaken actions that are mysterious to the rest of us. Some of them, you can't even believe how a person could do that. The person could do that because, within the construct of their own value system, that is to say, within the paradigm of their own conceptualization of self, their decisions and choices are entirely appropriate.

This idea has been formulated, or articulated in a single sentence: "No one does anything inappropriate." No one does anything inappropriate given their model of the world.

Most of us don't understand what conscience is really about. There's no such thing as conscience, because right and wrong don't exist. What does exist is the individual's ability to decide and to declare, to announce and to become who they imagine themselves to be. Once that declaration is made, and no matter how many times it's remade, you'll reset your target, you'll remake your announcement and declaration, and you'll readjust your internal guidance system and it will lead you right there. And, that's the internal guidance system that says yes or no to a particular decision, based on the largest choice you have made regarding who you think you are.

To Mr. Walsch, our conscience is the internal guidance system taking us to who we think we are; to the Hollywood film director who distinguishes between the inner voice and conscience, it is social right or wrong; to the young George Washington it is the voice of heaven. But to all of them, it is a voice separate from the internal voice we hear in every waking moment.

That internal voice of conscience we are all familiar with is the first "inner voice" we ever hear that is separate from our internal monologue and seems to be guiding us. Whatever its true source, we start on a path when we listen to it.

5. The Negative Voice of Conscience

Conscience has one telling characteristic: it's always negative. It says "No" rather than providing direction. Conscience admonishes us not to do wrong, but does not tell us what really is right. We are given moral choice. We evolve from a stimulus/response creature to a conscious moral being the first time we put our hand in the cookie jar and our voice of conscience says, "No!"

When conscience speaks, are we only recognizing the probability of anticipated consequences, are we feeling an inner moral sense, or are we listening to some higher wisdom? With our hand in the cookie jar, we are looking around for Mom. But what about claiming a questionable deduction on our income tax return, or perhaps responding to a request for help coming at an inconvenient time? At those times, the moral choice ("Should I or shouldn't I?") is not always so simple.

For some of life's choices, conscience seems no longer to serve as the best internal guidance. Our moral discernment reaches a point where the "soup" of conscience (heredity, environment, moral sense, guilt, practical wisdom, fear, experience, habit, authority, divinity) needs the clarification of a true inner voice. The inner voice generously provides POSITIVE direction and inspiration, whereas conscience can only say "No."

As expressed by J. B. Phillips in his book, YOUR GOD IS TOO SMALL:

To many people, conscience is almost all that they have by way of knowledge of God. This still small voice which makes them feel guilty and unhappy before, during, or after wrong-doing, is God speaking to them. It is this which, to some extent at least, controls their conduct. It is this which impels them to shoulder the irksome duty and choose the harder path.

Now no serious advocate of real adult religion would deny the function of conscience, or deny that its voice may at least give some inkling of the moral order that lies behind the obvious world in which we live. Yet to make conscience into God is a highly dangerous thing to do. For one thing . . . conscience is by no means an infallible guide; and for another it is extremely unlikely that we shall ever be moved to worship, love, and serve, a nagging inner voice that at worst spoils our pleasure and at best keeps us rather negatively on the path of virtue.

6. The Feeling of Conscience

In addition to "listening" to our conscience, we have all had the physical experience of conscience. We refer to it as a "pang of conscience." What is that feeling? For many it is a real physical feeling: a pain in the heart area, a sinking feeling in the pit of the stomach, a dryness in the mouth, a hot flash, a sharp pain. For all of us, this internal soundless message can be accompanied by feelings in our body. And so it can be with other internal voices that come to us.

7. Conscience and the Inner Voice

Conscience is usually not the Inner Voice, but the Inner Voice can manifest as conscience in its beginning phases.

— THE BOOK OF LIFE, BY MINERVA

When conscience becomes merely the learned voice of cultural morality, it may not be in perfect harmony with the inner voice. Some cultural demands, like the Spanish Inquisition or apartheid, have proven themselves to be less than uplifting, and certainly not timeless, universal truths. In addition, conscience can actually inhibit us from doing what we know is right by causing us to puzzle over what we have been told is wrong. As Shakespeare put it:

Thus conscience does make cowards of us all;
And thus the native hue of resolution

Is sicklied o'er with the pale cast of thought,
And enterprises of great pitch and moment
With this regard their currents turn awry,
And lose the name of action.

— HAMLET, ACT 3, SCENE 1

Through the reflexive response of conscience we arrive at the nearest shores of the territory of the inner voice. But when is conscience the divine inspiration of our inner voice instead of merely cultural conditioning? What do we do if we are uncertain about following our conscience, as opposed to another inner voice? To receive answers to such important questions, we must press forward into the realm of the inner voice.

HOW TO
Conscience

Think for a moment about the last time that you were
deliberately unkind to your mother, or had a verbal battle
with someone you love. Did you get a "pang of
conscience"? Do you know the feeling of conscience?

TRY IT!

- Drop a piece of trash in a public place and walk away. What feeling, urge or inner suggestion do you get?

How can we become more aware of our conscience? Many of us have masked our "feeling" abilities to the point that we can "feel" only our most extreme inner reactions, frequently our inner reactions to great personal loss. But we can easily revive our "feeling" sense and train ourselves to recognize when our bodies are trying to tell us something. By paying attention to signals from our bodies, we can become more aware of our sense of right and wrong.

TRY IT!

Take a sheet of paper with you to a place where you will not be disturbed. After taking three deep breaths from the pit of your stomach, say one of these statements out loud three times in a conversational voice and write down whatever feelings, twinges or conditions simultaneously occur in your body:

- I always speak the truth no matter what the consequences are.
- I am myself with my co-workers.
- I know what I want.
- I take full responsibility without blaming others for what's happening to me right now.
- I like myself.

Can you feel inner messages?

CHAPTER IV

Listening to the Inner Voice

What lies behind us and before us are small matters compared to what lies within us.

ESSAYS, BY RALPH WALDO EMERSON

Did you know that a doorway to the vast knowledge of the universe lies within you? In the beginning chapters, we explored the intuitive experiences that come to us all, and how they can lead us to a richer, more harmonious and creative life. When we go deeper within ourselves, we discover a doorway to a powerful source of insights and intelligence, and the key to this doorway is simply our ability to listen to the "still small voice" within us, our inner voice. In this chapter, we will examine the inner voice: what it is, what it sounds like, what it can tell us, and how we can "tune in to" it.

We often first hear our inner voice in a moment of great crisis, when we absolutely must know what to do and we have no answers readily available: We have a very sick child; we have just been in an automobile accident; our mate tells us he or she is leaving the relationship; we lose our job; or someone close to us dies. The "thousand natural shocks that flesh is heir to" cause us to search for solutions—and often come up with none. Where do we turn in such emergencies? Do we get on the telephone to a friend? Pray? Call a trained professional? Panic? Or do we listen within?

Let us look at how this voice came to Jim in a time of crisis:

> It happened at about 6:20 p.m. just as it was getting dark on a rainy Southern California winter evening. After driving into the street-level secured parking for my condominium complex, I got out of my car as the lattice-work metal garage door was sliding closed. When the door slid to within about four feet of closing, a person ran from the sidewalk into the garage. He was about 5'8", weighed about 140 pounds, and was in his early

twenties. I am much bigger than he was. He had a bandanna pulled up around his nose. As he ran past the closing gate, I heard him pump a round into the firing chamber of the pistol he was holding.

He ran toward me and demanded the gold Rolex I was wearing. I was not afraid but I was very alert. I was not at all thinking of being spiritual. I could not see him clearly because he was backlit by the fading daylight from the garage door. He repeated the demand. By this time he was nearly next to me. I took off the watch and gave it to him. I was standing by the open car door. At this point he said: "Turn around and lie down in the car." My first thought was that he wanted to kill me.

I paused for a moment trying to decide whether to attempt to overpower him or to, as I then thought, let him kill me. I decided to try to overpower him. When I got that thought, almost immediately I received a deep inner knowing that the reason for his demand was only that he wanted a clean getaway. I paused for an instant to consider whether to follow that inner feeling. He repeated the command that I turn around and lie down in the car. I decided to follow the inner knowing. At that point he simply ran away. There I stayed for a moment, completely unhurt, oddly relieved that the garish Rolex was out of my life, and feeling compassion for a young man whose life was supported by armed robbery. The emotion of the experience was gone within the hour.

I repeated the incident to a friend, who commented "You just bet your life on your inner voice."

1. What Is the Inner Voice?

Prayer is asking and meditation is listening for answers.

NANCY FREIER, PUBLISHER,
THE INNER VOICE, AN INTERNET MAGAZINE

We all pray, at one time or another–regularly as part of our daily lives, or at those times when the 747's wheels are about to touch down, or when the baby's due, or when the occurrence of something very dear to us seems to depend upon chance. Why do we pray? Because we think, or hope, or believe that God can hear us and grant our request, "hear" our prayers. How do we pray? By mentally forming the words or feeling we want to communicate to God: "Please God, let my daughter's fever break." But why do we "speak" to God by forming thoughts within us? Because intuitively that's where we know God is. Indeed, all great religions contain some belief that God is within each of us:

Islamic: "I am in your souls. Why see ye not? In every breath of yours, I am."

Buddhist: "Every being has the Buddha Nature. This is the self."

Shinto: "The human mind, partaking of divinity, is an abode of the Deity, which is the spiritual essence. There exists no higher Deity outside the human mind."

Hindu: "I am the True, the Real, Brahma. That thou art also. The heart of man is the abode of God."

Christian: "The kingdom of God does not come with observation; nor will they say, 'See here!' or 'See there!' For indeed, the kingdom of God is within you."   LUKE 17:20
"Do you not know that you are the temple of God and that the Spirit of God dwells in you?" 1 CORINTHIANS 3:16

For most people, prayer is a one-way, internal discussion with the God within them. To read prayers out of prayer books is to discover a great line of praises, requests, entreaties, confessions and other appeals. However, occasionally we find references to the experiences of people having God respond to them. We talk and talk and talk to God–quite suddenly, God says something back! That is what we mean by the "inner voice," the voice of a returned prayer, an answered question, and all the accompanying joy and peace that attend the truth.

Is it possible that an all-powerful God actually speaks to human beings? The world's enduring religions were founded and fueled by people (Zoroaster, Lao-Tze, the Hebrew prophets, Jesus, Mohammed, St. Paul, St. Augustine and others) who heard God speak to them from within. Sacred writing and scriptures are replete with stories of God speaking to human beings. Indeed, if we were too insignificant to God for him to bother to speak to us, why did he create us? What loving parent forgoes the opportunity to speak with his or her children?

Philosophical and religious traditions throughout the world and over many centuries have all contained some concept of the inner voice speaking to individual human beings. It has been called the Holy Spirit, the Breath, the I AM, the "still small voice." And it is available to all of us ("My sheep hear My voice"), not just to holy men. Fundamentally, the inner voice is each individual's communication from the divine presence within.

We have tried to identify what makes these two-way conversations possible between God and humankind and have discovered a few recurring themes. Often when people are desperate for an answer and ask forcefully, then wait and LISTEN intently, there is a response. The normal internal monologue that we hear in our thoughts changes dramatically. It is as if we were being spoken to. Here's how Ralph Waldo Emerson experienced his inner voice:

> Man begins to hear a voice that fills the heavens and the earth saying that God is within himself; that THERE is the celestial host. I find this amazing revelation of my immediate relation to God a solution of all the doubts that oppressed me. I recognize the distinction of the outer and inner self; the double consciousness that within this erring, passionate, mortal self sits a supreme, calm, immortal mind, whose powers I do not know; but it is stronger than I; it is wiser than

I; it never reproved me in any wrong; I seek counsel of it in my doubts; I repair to it in my dangers; I pray to it in my undertakings. It seems to me to be the face which the Creator uncovers to his child.

FROM THE WORKS OF RALPH WALDO EMERSON, edited by Richard Garnett

Once this voice has been heard and acknowledged as an important aspect of your consciousness, you return again and again to the source of this wisdom within. It brings such peace to your life that you long for more of the upliftment it provides. Eventually, you come to rely on this voice within as a guide by which you live your life.

> Let a man return into his own self, and there in the center of his soul, let him wait upon God, as one who listens to another speaking from a high tower, as though he had God in

his heart, as though in the whole of creation there was only God and his soul.

ST. PETER OF ALCANTARA, quoted in THE MYSTIC VISION, BY HARVEY BARING

2. What Does the Inner Voice Sound Like?

...And, behold, the LORD passed by, and a great and strong wind rent the mountains, and broke in pieces the rocks before the LORD; but the LORD was not in the wind: and after the wind an earthquake; but the LORD was not in the earthquake.
And after the earthquake a fire; but the LORD was not in the fire; and after the fire a still small voice.

I KINGS 19:11

This Biblical reference to the "still small voice" has been an enigma to people who have not yet recognized an inner voice. But it is a completely clear and understandable phrase to those who have "heard." How can a voice be "still"? How can the voice of truth be "small"? These seeming contradictions are quite understandable to those in contact with their inner voice. The quiet, but totally memorable, voice of truth is as gentle as a whisper, but as enduring as a water-smoothed river rock.

We each carry on an internal monologue, and for many people the inner voice occurs as part of that monologue or in the same tones as their monologue. For other people, and for the same people at other times, the inner voice comes as a deep inner knowing or a feeling of truth. Although some hear the inner voice so profoundly as to think it audible, it is not the voice of a strange person in your head or the voice of your frenetic self or your urgent self. It is, however, a peaceful knowing expression in the inner language that we normally speak. It is not the voice of Charlton Heston parting the Red Sea that you hear, but it is the voice that you are familiar with, speaking to you with authority; it is "amazing grace, how sweet the sound."

As expressed to us in correspondence by Robert Wall Crary, author of THE STILL SMALL VOICE:

> The Inner Voice comes to everyone in absolute silence. It comes as frequencies of Light, like radio waves into a radio, coming from a radio transmitter or broadcasting station. These frequencies are the Light of God, coming to each and every human being through his own spiritual Counterpart within him. So they come as Light waves within him, hence in silence.
>
> Only when the conscious mind of anyone responds sufficiently to this Light, lifting his vibrations of Light to synchronize with this Light, which is the Spirit of God within him, can he tune into these frequencies and receive the messages they bear.

3. On First Hearing an Inner Voice

Your ears shall hear a word behind you, saying, "This is the way, walk in it ...."

ISAIAH 30:21

The inner voice is universal, everyone has one. Many persons have written about first hearing their inner voice. Some first experiences have come in times of great crisis; some have come from conscious attempts to seek inner guidance for the first time. Here are two examples of first experiences with the inner voice.

Eileen Cady was one of the founders of Findhorn, an ecologically advanced community in Scotland, in the 1960s.

Her first experience with the inner voice was as follows:

> ... God was still somewhat like the Father, separate and above us, reaching down to help. But gradually I have come to understand what it means to find that same God within myself. The first time I heard this voice was in 1953 when Peter and I were visiting Glastonbury, a center of spiritual power in England. I was sitting in the stillness of a small private sanctuary there, when I heard a voice–a very clear voice–within me. I had never experienced anything like that before. It simply said, "Be still and know that I am God." What is this? I thought. Am I going mad? I had been brought up in the Church of England and learned in Sunday school about the "still small voice within"–but when you actually hear a voice, it's a different matter. I was really quite shocked because it was so clear.

I don't want to give the idea that this just happened without any preparation. There had been a great deal of spiritual training leading up to that point. Yet hearing this voice was totally unexpected. Following the experience, I went through a painful period of conflict and tension when I kept hearing many different voices, all battling to be first. I just kept listening and listening until I heard one clear voice again, and then the others disappeared.

"What greater or more wonderful relationship could a man ask for than the knowledge that he is truly one with me, that I am in you and you are in me?" Accepting the reality of this oneness came slowly. In fact, at first I felt it was audacious even to speak of such a thing. Yet, I couldn't deny my experience. I know that God is within each one of us, within everything. I feel that the church teaches about the God outside of us, but that's the

same God as the one within ....
Eventually receiving guidance from the
voice of God became the most natural
thing in the world.

THE FINDHORN GARDEN BY THE FINDHORN
COMMUNITY, NARRATIVE BY EILEEN CADY

Gerald Jampolsky, M.D., was a very successful child and adult psychiatrist who felt like a failure inside. He was suffering from a "spiritual deprivation" which no physical success could fill.

I certainly wasn't looking for a personal
transformation, a spiritual transformation, or
God. I'd been a militant atheist all my life,
ever since high school when a dear friend
was killed in an automobile accident. In
1975, my life was in great chaos. My twenty-
year marriage had ended in a very painful
divorce. I became an alcoholic. I had
developed an incapacitating back pain, called

degenerative back syndrome. And even my
medical license was in jeopardy from a drunk
driving incident. It was about this time that a
friend of mine presented me with a Xerox
copy of these three books called A Course in
Miracles. I asked, "Well, what are they
about?" "It's about spiritual transformation."
"Well, I'm not interested in any of that stuff.
Thank you, but no thanks." She was very
insistent, and just to get her off my back I
said, "Okay, I'll read just one page." What
happened was one of the most amazing
experiences of my life. I heard a little inner
voice saying, "Physician, heal thyself. This is
your way home."

— LOVE IS LETTING GO OF FEAR (AUDIO PRO-
GRAM) BY GERALD G. JAMPOLSKY, M.D.

4. How Do You Access the Inner Voice?

There are some simple steps to accessing the inner voice. Reading these steps will not produce results. Only by doing them will you take the idea of the inner voice to the level of experience. We suggest that you finish reading the chapter and then come back to the box below, put the book down and take these simple steps to the inner voice.

> *INNER VOICE ACCESS STEPS:*
> - *Know that you are worthy to hear.*
>   - *Formulate a question.*
>   - *Quiet the mind.*
>   - *Anticipate hearing.*
> - *Listen intently and patiently.*
>   - *Pay attention to whatever you get.*
>   - *Write down your answer.*

That is all there is to it. We will consider each of these steps in detail.

A. You Are Worthy

The first step to hearing the inner voice is to accept the fact that you are worthy to have an inner voice speak to you. Throughout history, man has devised proxies to use to disguise the fact that part of our self is all-knowing and capable of delivering specific answers to specific questions. The I Ching, tarot cards, fortune-telling and other forms of specific divination have all relied upon some interface between the individual and his inner knowing. The first step in listening, then, is simply to accept the fact that you are worthy to be spoken to directly by God; without the intervention of a shaman or intermediary. The worthiness of each of us is well described in this seventeenth-century poem by George Herbert:

THE SACRED MARRIAGE

Love bade me welcome;
yet my soul drew back,
Guilty of dust and sin.
But quick-ey'd Love,
observing me grow slack
From my first entrance in,
Drew nearer to me, sweetly questioning
If I lack'd any thing.
"A guest," I answered,
"worthy to be here:"
Love said, "You shall be he."
I, the unkind, the ungrateful?
Ah, my dear,
I cannot look on thee."
Love took my hand and smiling did reply,
"Who made the eyes but I?"
"Truth, Lord; but I have marr'd them:
let my shame
Go where it doth deserve."
"And know you not," says Love,
"who bore the blame?"

"My dear, then I will serve."
"You must sit down," says Love,
"And taste my meat."
So I did sit and eat.

Look at it from God's point of view: Do you want to and like to speak to your own children? God, whose scripture tells us that He made us in His image and likeness, has usually been likened to a parent. What parent does not want to speak to his or her children? Do you want to speak to your children only when they've been good and not when they've been bad? All parents have had the experience of wanting and needing to love their children at precisely the points when the children are the "baddest" and the neediest of the parents' love. Why should God be any different? A component of your feeling of worthiness to hear the voice of God is God's own desire to communicate with you.

In one of his *CONVERSATIONS WITH GOD*, Neale Donald Walsch records God as saying:

> This is the root of every problem you experience in your life—for you do not consider yourself worthy enough to be spoken to by God. Good heavens, how can you ever expect to hear My voice if you don't imagine yourself to be deserving enough even to be spoken to? I tell you this: I am performing a miracle right now. For not only am I speaking to you, but to every person who has picked up this book and is reading these words. To each of them am I now speaking. I know who every one of them is. I know now who will find their way to these words—and I know that (just as with all My other communications) some will be able to hear—and some will be able only to listen, but will hear nothing.

Finally, when we are considering our own worthiness to be spoken to by the Creator of the universe, looking at the following example from the life of Adolf Hitler (from *I KNOW THESE DICTATORS* by George Ward Price) can give us a perspective on God's universal concern for us all:

> Then, too, Hitler has reported several incidents during the [First World] war which proved to him that he was under Divine protection. The most startling of these is the following:
> "I was eating my dinner in a trench with several comrades. Suddenly a voice seemed to be saying to me, 'Get up and go over there.' It was so clear and insistent that I obeyed automatically, as if it had been a military order. I rose at once to my feet and walked twenty yards along the trench carrying my dinner in its tin can with me. Then I sat down to go on

eating, my mind being once more at rest. Hardly had I done so when a flash and deafening report came from the part of the trench I had just left. A stray shell had burst over the group in which I had been sitting, and every member of it was killed."

If Hitler was given access to an inner voice, aren't we as worthy?

I am closer to you than yourself,

Than your soul, than your own breath.

Why do you not see me?

Why do you not hear me?

IBN AL ARABI,

FROM STUDIES IN ISLAMIC MYSTICISM

B. Formulate the Question

How does one formulate the questions to ask the inner voice? Trial lawyers have known for many years that he who frames the question often controls the answer. A classic example of such a question is: "Are you still beating your wife?" A "no" answer (even from someone who never beat his wife) can be interpreted to mean that, although you are no longer doing so, you once did beat your wife. The question makes an assumption (that you once beat your wife) that any answer will affirm, whether the wife beating is actually true or not. Because framing the question can frame the answer, asking a clear question in a neutral way is fundamental to getting a clear answer.

We suggest that inner voice questions stand the best chance of useful answers when they are non-assuming, unambiguous, objective, specific and complete. We will examine each of these qualities below, but the "fix" for a problematic question is usually simply to "break it down" into a series of more analytically focused questions. For example, the question, "Do I place my son in a drug rehabilitation program for his behavior problems?" could be broken down into separate questions such as: "Does my son have a drug problem?" "Is it in the best interests of all concerned that he be in a drug rehabilitation program?" and so forth.

The first step in getting an unambiguous answer is to ask an unambiguous question. The least ambiguous questions are those calling only for a "yes" or "no" answer, so that's the starting point. "Should we hire Karen to teach the history course next fall, or should we consider someone else, either from the current staff or from the outside?" might be rephrased: "Is it in the best interests of all concerned that Karen teach the history course next fall?"

However, even "yes" and "no" questions must not be vague, as reflected in Ellen's following experience:

> A very close friend asked for my help in asking the inner voice a question about her relationship with her boyfriend. The question she sought an answer to was: "Should I stay with Bill?" When she asked that question of her inner voice, the answers she got were always universal, and not too satisfying to her: "always love your friends" and "stay close to those you love."
>
> We talked, and I told her that only she could get answers pertinent to her life from her inner voice, but that the phrasing of her question could be the problem. Does "Should I stay with Bill?" mean "live in the same house?" "romantic relationship?" "platonic connection?" As we talked, it was clear that my friend had mixed feelings about the impact of their sexual relationship on Bill's life. Bill had

never had children, and my friend could no longer have children: was her physical relationship with Bill preventing his meeting the ultimate mother of his children? My friend also felt somewhat threatened by Bill's occasional glances at other women.

After we talked, it became clear that my friend's underlying concern was: "Is it in the best interests of all concerned that I withdraw myself from my sexual relationship with Bill?" The answer she got was: "Not at this time." This answer satisfied her questions and worked for them for several years.

Good questions are specific. "What should I do with my life?" might not produce a specific answer. Similarly, "Do I go along with my spouse's plan to purchase this house?" might not produce as useful an answer as: "Do I object to buying this house?"

Being neutral or objective in asking the question, and not asking leading questions ("I can drink this double scotch, can't I?") is also important. Consider the following approach of Patricia Jepsen Chuse, a spiritual teacher:

> I do think that when you are going for specific information, you have to make it very, very, very clear. Be very specific as to what your question is, because it's how you place that question, is how it's going to come back.
>
> Where is that question coming from in you? Is it coming from a place of anxiety and fear? Is it coming from a desire for your life to be better, or is it coming from a sense of intuitive prodding that is seemingly saying, "I've got to ask this question. I'm not sure why, but I know I must and the answer will be here." Then, that's the place where you are really working in the Spirit.

One of the best things I can say about asking a question, is try to clear yourself of fear and anxiety, because if you have a lot of emotions around, for the most part the answers are not going to be truthful, not going to be clear, and they're probably not coming from the inner voice. We can make up stuff to make things better for us. Often we do that. That's one of the things that happens with the inner voice. Sometimes people get upset–they say "I didn't get my inner voice direction right, I've failed." We continually must refine that inner voice, and not get upset at all. This is a fascinating sphere to be in, in a sense. If you find that you might have fantasized a little bit, you might have brought something up from your subconscious that might have interfered with the directions, that's okay, that happens. Go back and try again.

We suggest two steps to establishing your neutrality as to the result of your question. Ask yourself these questions:

1. Is the guidance I am seeking consistent with the good of the whole? Is it guidance that will benefit mankind?
2. Have I released my attachment to the result of the requested guidance? Have I refrained from coloring the request or from anticipating a particular answer? Have I established my unconcern for the direction that the inner voice directs me to take?

For example, suppose that you are choosing between two job opportunities. Your first question may be: "Which job does the universe want me in at this time?" As you evaluate the choices, you might ask yourself, "What is my role in taking this job?" and "Which job would best serve the good of the whole, judged from the viewpoint of the whole and not from the point of view of myself?" When the answer comes, that is the job to take.

If your feeling about one of several choices is so strong that objectivity is virtually impossible, it is probably better not even to go through the exercise of asking the inner voice about the choice, because the exercise will likely be futile.

In a free-will universe, the inner voice is not likely to override the free choice already made.

The questions most likely to produce complete answers are also complete questions. ("Is this decision best for me?" versus "Is this decision best for all concerned?" "Can we make money on this?" versus "Is this best for the next seven generations?")

Some questions seem rarely to produce useful answers:

- "When will I be loved?"

- "How can I get a nice car like that?"

- "How much will I receive for this?"

- "When will my bad luck change?"

Perhaps time and material value have little meaning to the inner voice. On the other hand, some questions seem frequently to produce reliable answers:

- "What was my lesson in this experience?"

- "Have I released my attachment to a particular result?"

- "What is my role in this situation?"

- "Do I take this project on?"

- "What do I say to the person who has asked me for my advice?"

- "What is the most loving response to that?"

- "How do I today approach the person I had difficulty with yesterday?"

- "What is my next step in completing this project?"

Generally, the questions that seem to get answers are the sincere questions, asked when we are at a loss for the right direction and are seeking real guidance. When we think that no answer is possible, but are open to unexpected directions, the answers seem to come. And it is the frequent experience of many asking such questions that:

1. they think when they ask that they won't get any answer at all;
2. they actually get an answer;
3. their minds immediately negate the answer received as unimportant, as too simplistic or as just the workings of their mind;
4. the answer works perfectly to answer the question.

What questions should we ask our inner voice? We may feel that the inner voice is sacred and should be asked only sacred questions about weighty subjects in our lives. But what is sacred? What is weighty? In a similar vein, we may feel that our task in life is to do God's work. However, what is God's work but the work He placed before us to do? If the work was unimportant, why did God give it to us to do? Similarly, if the questions we face, however small, are not important to God, why does He bother to give them to us to resolve? In a universe where the Bible tells us (at Luke 12:7) that "even the very hairs of your head are all numbered," the "mundane" merits the assistance of the inner voice as much as the "profound."

As Neale Donald Walsch puts it:

> First of all, I've come to understand that there's no difference between the mundane and the profound, and that the biggest mistake we make is categorizing things as one or the other. . . . every decision and choice we make . . . every movement or action we take, is an announcement and a declaration of who we are. . . . I find in fact that the smallest choices hold the largest keys to who we create ourselves as being. . . . Do I drink tap water, or is it bottled water? Do I eat meat, or no red meat and just poultry, or no meat at all? Do I wear white or black? . . . Do I go to plays or do I see Sylvester Stallone in movies shooting people apart again? How do I spend the days and times of my life? Who do I accept phone calls from? How do I speak to people? What words do I chose? What tone of voice am I going to use here in this thirty seconds? The tiniest, tiniest choices create . . . a projection into the universe of who I imagine myself to be. . . . there's no such thing as mundane choices. . . . I've learned that it is really in the contemplation of those minute decisions in life that the joy and the celebration of the creation itself is found. . . I create for myself . . . and make an active choice, in this moment now. As I make that choice, I listen to the voice within. . . . Masters take great care in the small things because they know that mountains are made of pebbles.

So ask away! You will find that the inner voice does not refuse sincere requests for guidance on the "tiniest" of subjects.

Ask, and it will be given to you; seek, and you will find; knock, and it will be opened to you. For everyone who asks receives, and he who seeks finds, and to him who knocks it will be opened.   MATTHEW 7:7

> *EFFECTIVE INNER VOICE*
> *QUESTIONS ARE:*
> - *non-assuming*
> - *unambiguous*
> - *objective*
> - *specific*
> - *complete*

C. Quiet the Conscious Mind

Be still and know that I am God....

PSALMS 46:10

The next step in listening to the inner voice is to slow down the constant flow of mental thoughts coursing through our waking mind, to quiet our mind. Why is it necessary to turn down the volume? Simply because we cannot tune in to the divine if we are tuned in to the cacophony.

Many people find that the easiest way to quiet the mind is through meditation. We may react to the suggestion of meditation by protesting that we do not know how to meditate or do not think that we are able to meditate. But every person (good or bad, spiritual or scoundrel) every day quiets the mind when going to sleep. We don't just go from the state of being fully awake to the state of being fully asleep; we first consciously quiet our mind. Quieting the mind, and yet remaining awake–"falling awake"–is really all there is to meditation.

But there are other ways people have used throughout history to quiet the mind. One is to take a walk with nowhere in particular to go. This has been so effective an introduction into contemplative states that the cathedral builders in medieval Europe often patterned a circular labyrinth, or single-path maze, in stone on the floor of the church, like the one that has been in continuous use since 1201 A.D. in the cathedral at Chartres, outside of Paris. This ancient spiral induces a sort of "walking meditation," which is the way in which the labyrinth at Grace Cathedral in San Francisco is used today. People find that answers come when they walk its circular path.

Another way to quiet the mind is simply to be beside the water.

> Say you are in the country; in some high land of lakes. Take almost any path you please, and ten to one it carries you down in a dale, and leaves you there by a pool in the stream.

> There is magic in it. Let the most absent-minded of men be plunged in his deepest reveries—stand that man on his legs, set his feet a-going, and he will infallibly lead you to water .... Yes, as everyone knows, meditation and water are wedded for ever.
>
> MOBY DICK BY HERMAN MELVILLE

Take a look for yourself; go down to the beach. What do you see? Among the children and the revelers you will always find the contemplative gazing out over the water, staring silently into the vastness of their souls.

The experience of quieting the mind has been mapped in detail. It has been found that in an "alpha state" of wakeful relaxation, our electrical brain waves slow to eight to thirteen cycles per second. This occurs just before falling asleep and in meditation, as well as in jogging, showering, commuting to work, fishing, gardening, walking and any activity that requires very little focused brain activity. Under these circumstances, the brain is free to reach out and communicate with the rest of the universe.

> When I came into the state between sleep and wakefulness, I had an impression that an indescribably beautiful voice was speaking words of encouragement: "You are my beloved daughter in whom I am well pleased." When I came into full wakefulness it seemed as though a celestial orchestra had just finished playing in the station, with its echoes still lingering on. I walked out into the cold morning, but I felt warm. I walked along the cement sidewalk, but I felt I was walking on clouds. The feeling of living in harmony with divine purpose has never left me.
>
> PEACE PILGRIM:
> HER LIFE AND WORKS IN HER OWN WORDS,
> BY FRIENDS OF PEACE PILGRIM

The ways of quieting the mind are as varied as there are human beings to exercise them. Consider the following two:

Tom Edwards, secondary school educator:

> I have a natural ability to just go into a meditative state and I can get there. I don't know how I do it and I don't need to know, but it just happens. So, I just do it, and it's becoming more and more natural to do it.

Jack Hart, a teacher of Higher Mind studies:

> The inner voice seems to happen more just when I'm at ease and living my life naturally. That can be happening when I'm meditating, or while I'm skiing, or while I'm falling asleep, or while I'm sleeping. It's a different kind of awareness than while I'm talking. It doesn't seem that it's more specific to when I'm

meditating or to when I'm not meditating. It seems like it's there all the time. My awareness of it can happen at any kind of time. I guess I do know that if I have to give a talk, it most frequently becomes clear to me how to give the talk when I'm taking a shower. So, it seems that in the shower is where some real awareness comes. There is some process that I'm not overthinking; I'm not getting in the way of my thought. I'm sort of scrubbing down my body, and yet, it's something that I'm thinking about usually at the time that I go in there. But, I've stopped sort of focusing on it and then it just seems to be able to flow in. Although, sometimes it does happen when I'm focusing on it too.

D. Anticipate Hearing

Let us assume that you have identified a burning question. You are seated and quiet and you begin to tell yourself, "this is a ridiculous exercise; I'll never get any answers this way; I should know better." At this point you have the choice to stop the exercise or to change your mental attitude to one of anticipation. By anticipation, we mean looking forward to a successful experience, desiring and expecting clear and helpful insights. Anticipation carries with it some excitement at what possibility lies ahead. You are open and receptive without preconceived ideas–childlike almost. You are poised to hear and learn.

… be ye as little children… MATTHEW 18:3

E. Listen Intently and Patiently

I ask a question and I get an answer in a feeling about an hour later.

— KATE, NINE YEARS OLD

The temptation for the mind to wander when we have asked our inner voice a question is overwhelming. Let it! But also be alert to whatever comes, whenever it comes. We have all had the experience of trying to remember the name of the company that repaired the gate, or the access code to the voicemail box, or the person who knew how to book reasonable fares to New York. And we have all had the experience that, if we just forget about it, the elusive information will later suddenly pop into our minds when we least expect it, when we are washing our hands, or walking the dog, or watching the news. How often have we each said, "It'll come to me." It is the same with listening to the inner voice: Do it intently, but only in the sense that you are waiting for the answer to a particular question you have asked, not forcing the answer or thinking about nothing else until the answer comes. Patience.

We have considered the inner voice's communicating with us as "words" that we "listen to" coming into our mind, but that is only one way that the inner voice can communicate with us. In what other ways can the inner voice's communications come to us? Thomas Armstrong in his book 7 KINDS OF SMART, identified seven different kinds of intelligence (linguistic intelligence, a way with words; kinesthetic intelligence, the dancer's grace; spatial intelligence, the architect's eye; musical intelligence, the Mozart intelligence; mathematical intelligence, Stephen Hawking's abstract perception of time; interpersonal intelligence, that ability instinctively to understand what other people want; and intrapersonal intelligence, the ability to draw wisdom from within). The inner voice can come to us through any of those forms of intelligence and frequently comes to the same person through different avenues. In addition, our awareness of "knowing" something can come to us in words, in a feeling, in thought pictures (visualizations, dreams or daydreams), as a "proto-thought" (or the kernel of a thought which, upon reflection, links together all parts of the entire concept summarized in the initial thought), as the intellectual realization of a "knowing," and in many other ways. The inner voice can also use such avenues to our consciousness. Thus, listening intently includes being aware of "knowing" in all of the different ways that it can, and frequently does, come to us.

F. Pay Attention to Whatever You Get

There are many answers you have received, but have not yet heard.

A COURSE IN MIRACLES

Surprisingly often, the most difficult aspect of listening to the inner voice is actually believing in what we get. The answers seem too simple to be true: "Why didn't I think of that before?" Or the answers can seem as if we are just "making them up," as if our minds are filling in the blanks with fantasy and not something divine. That's exactly what it should feel like: that teetering on the edge of credibility, that sensing the gossamer strands of a separate reality. Remember, the divine world is much finer, much faster, much more elusive than our material plane. The greatest truths of the inner voice "come with the dust and are gone with the wind." So, if it feels as if you're making your answers up, write them down and apply the tests of discernment discussed in the next chapter, to see whether, as in nearly all profound experiences, you have just "entertained an angel unawares."

G. Write It Down

Why write it down? It is our common experience that writing something down has the effect of crystallizing it for us, helping us to retain it in our minds long after the writing is discarded, giving the thought credibility to our consciousness. And so it is with the inner voice: its words seem so simple, so mundane, so easy to forget; but when we write its words down and look at them later we see how profound they really are.

5. Inner Geography–the Ear of Your Heart

> The heart has its reasons which reason knows
> nothing of.   BLAISE PASCAL

It can be helpful in inner listening to understand your own inner geography. That is, we have the capability of putting our consciousness wherever we want in our bodies, and ultimately outside of our bodies. Most of us keep our consciousness in our brains. But with simple exercises it is possible to put your consciousness in your elbow or your leg or your heart. (If you doubt this, think of where your consciousness went the last time you burned your finger!) We suggest that putting your consciousness into your heart instead of your brain may be a way more easily to access the inner voice in your internal geography.

Many people have had the experience of coming to understand the concept of inner geography. Here's how Nancy Freier, publisher of THE INNER VOICE, an Internet magazine, explains it:

> To answer this, listen carefully because
> this isn't easy to explain. To me, it's a

combination of my mind with my heart, and then I'm going to have to say it's a voice coming from the throat area. Although it's inside, it's an audible voice and is somehow combined with the voice that's in your head to whatever feeling is going on in your heart. It's a combination of that mental energy with the heart . . . coming through the throat because that's where we speak. It is a heart/mind energy coming through in words. If your heart could talk, that's how I would have to describe it.

Indeed, we all naturally "listen" at times with the consciousness in our hearts, as we can all "feel" the message expressed in a favorite love song:

Now the village mission bells are softly ringing.
If you listen with your heart, you'll hear them singing,

"Vaya con Dios my darling, May God be with you my love."

The ear of the heart can be a powerful receiver of the inner voice.

6. Group Guidance

. . . where two or three are gathered together in My name, I am there in the midst of them.
MATTHEW 18:20

When a group of people become silent together and listen for direction or an answer to a shared question, group guidance is possible, and it is the universal experience of such groups that the advice is clearer and more complete because it is done in a group.

The Quaker tradition was founded upon this principle. In 1647, founder George Fox was seeking answers to spiritual questions without success. One day, he heard a voice saying: "There is one, even Jesus Christ, that can speak to thy condition," after which he began his dialogue with Christ, which led to the founding of the Society of Friends, or the Quakers. Quaker worship services are silent gatherings without liturgy or supervision, which allows the believers to listen for that "still small voice" to lead them.

Contemporary nonreligious groups, small businesses and private schools have begun to use group meditation as a shortcut to decision making, since it avoids much haggling, politics and pointmaking. Consider the experience of Richard Handley, a private high-school administrator:

> Quite often we are troubled by what to do with a particular student. Teenagers can go through periods of outrageous behaviors, and, if they are helped through such periods, can come out as wonderful human beings, all to the benefit of the teenager exhibiting the behavior, the other students and the school. On the other hand, some teenagers' outrageous behaviors can set a negative tone for an entire school, and, in effect, bring the whole school to its knees.
>
> Whenever we do not know what to do with a particular student exhibiting outrageous behavior, the administrators and a few staff members in our private high school sit quietly together and ask for guidance in our decision making. We ask for the solution that is best for the whole school, as well as the student.
>
> In eight years we have never had conflicting guidance in the group. We all seem to receive a different piece of the pie. Together, the guidance addresses all of our concerns and provides a complete picture of the solution. Thus, we may learn from the math teacher that the parents should be asked to have a

conference, the philosophical basis for a sound decision may come through another teacher, and so forth.

Consider also the following experience of a group working together. This group had no access to the information they needed to solve the problem, so, working together, they had to pull it out of themselves. In the words of a Bennington College coed:

A group of friends were driving through Arizona. We were in two cars, and we got separated somehow, and it was not a good thing really because there were people in both cars that needed to reconnect to go to the next location, separate from each other. We didn't all live in the same place, we lived hours and hours apart. So, two of my friends and I were in one car, and, although it felt really hopeless, we said: "Okay, we can find them. Let's use our combined forces to do this." One of the friends played with runes[1]. I don't know a whole lot about them, but I think that, if you're smart, you can use them as almost just a visual articulation of the inner voice. We were doing the runes and my friends asked me "What are you sensing? What do you get, where are they?" So, I tuned in to my inner voice, and I got that they were going to stop at a crossroads point. My friend then picked a rune, and the rune said that was about crossroads. It was absolutely about crossroads. So, we said: "Okay, we're onto something." We picked another rune, and what we got was that they were at the point of entrances, minute entrances. It was really strange, we couldn't figure out what that was about. Then, all of a sudden, I got this very strong sense, this

[1] Runes, ancient Nordic pre-alphabetic symbols of mystical significance, originally carved on stones, are currently used like Tarot cards to suggest answers to questions.

very strong picture of them at a restaurant. So, we opened up a map, and we were looking at where there was a crossroads. At the same time, we all said: "Needles! They're at Needles." It was the weirdest thing, because there's a lot of different crossroads that you could have gone to, but we all had a strong sense—I think partly, when we got the thing about openings, small openings, we all just finally said "Oh, Needles." We immediately drove to Needles, California, and there was a restaurant right at the first freeway off-ramp. We got off and went into the restaurant and there they were, sitting in a booth. So, that was really fun. That was really fun.

7. Ramifications of Listening to the Inner Voice

We do not mind coming to Mass
to sing hymns,
to organize celebrations,
putting on our Sunday best,
giving offerings.
But to sit down
and listen to God
in the quiet of the evening
in our room
or on a mountaintop,
as Jesus did,
that is too dangerous,
too hazardous.
Just think what God
might ask us to do.

CHRIST, THE DIVINE NETWORK
BY JOSEPH G. DONDERS

Listening to the inner voice is more than just an intellectual or spiritual exercise. The experience of listeners is that, as the inner voice gets stronger, our lives begin to change in accordance with the messages. We begin to experience in life what the messages reveal.

The more faithfully you listen to the voice within you, the better you will hear what is sounding outside. And only he who listens can speak. Is this the starting point of the road towards the union of your two dreams—to be allowed in clarity of mind to mirror life and in purity of heart to mold it?

MARKINGS BY DAG HAMMERSKJOLD

When the directions received are followed, the inner voice becomes stronger and stronger. If the directions given are not followed, the voice becomes weaker—and may we suggest this is so because of the Universe's respect for the free will of the individual? The inner voice will not shout louder if we are covering our ears.

... every one of us has a special place in the Life Pattern, and no two people have exactly the same part to play in God's plan. There is a guidance which comes from within to all who listen. Through this guidance each one will feel drawn to some part in the scheme of things.

God's laws can be known from within, but they can also be known from without, as they have been spoken of by all great religious teachers. God's guidance can only be known from within.

We must remain open to God's guidance. God never guides us to break divine law, and if such a negative guidance comes to us we can be sure it is not from God. It is up to us to keep our lives steadfastly in harmony with divine law, which is the same for all of us. Only insofar as we remain in harmony with divine law do good things come to us.

When you come into this world your jobs in the divine plan are there. They just need to be realized and lived. If you do not yet know where you fit, I suggest that you try seeking it in receptive silence. I used to walk amid the beauties of nature, just receptive and silent, and wonderful insights would come to me.

PEACE PILGRIM:
HER LIFE AND WORKS IN HER OWN WORDS,
BY FRIENDS OF PEACE PILGRIM

And what happens to those of us who are not quiet enough to hear our inner voice? We do not receive the inspirations, and we do not have the eyes to see the evidence of the harmony in the universe. The richness, color and passion in life comes from heeding that inner voice. We do not always understand the fountain of creativity and ideas flowing within us, but without it, our lives, in the words of Hamlet, are "weary, flat, stale and unprofitable."

Finally, there seems to be an undeniable connection between the inner voice and healing, a healing of the heart. Nancy Freier, publisher of *THE INNER VOICE*, an Internet magazine, comments:

> I believe that the intention of the Inner Voice is to heal hearts. When we do that we also heal our minds and bodies. It's all rolled into one. My particular area of expertise is healing the heart because I think that's where our pain is; and if we can heal that, our lives can become happier and we can bypass disease. I think it's important for the Inner Voice to keep the message of love flowing through the heart because then you just can't be miserable. You can't be joyful and unhappy at the same time and joy springs from love flowing through the heart.

The connection between the inner voice and healing is echoed in the life of Mother Teresa. Mother Teresa was the mischievous child of an Albanian grocer and his wife. She grew up in Skopje, a culturally diverse Macedonian city with mosques, Catholic cathedrals, and Eastern Orthodox churches. She became a nun, joined a missionary order and for seventeen years was a gifted geography teacher in a girls' school in Calcutta, India. One day, while riding a train, she felt God call her to serve the poorest of the poor on the streets of Calcutta. Mother Teresa was thirty-eight when she got permission from the church to start a new order called the Missionaries of Charity. With no money, no companions and no plan, she proceeded to pick up her first dying man. She said the smell was terrible and that worms had already gotten to him when she began to wash him. But if she hadn't been able to pick him up, she would never have picked up the next 42,000.

As you become more and more attuned to this inner voice, your life begins to move in that direction. The voice becomes a more vital and dynamic part of your everyday life. It can become the guiding principle of your life.

> Why did Gautama once sit down beneath the bo tree in his greatest hour when he received enlightenment? He had heard a voice, a voice in his own heart ...which commanded him to seek rest under this tree ... he had listened to the voice. To obey no other external command, only the voice, to be prepared—that was good, that was necessary. Nothing else was necessary.
>
> FROM SIDDHARTHA, BY HERMANN HESSE

HOW TO
Listening To The Inner Voice

Quiet places are the most conducive environments for listening to the inner voice. Throughout history, people have found places that seem to help in quieting the mind–the ocean, a city park, gardens, a revered place in the home. In fact, one of the easiest places to quiet the mind, to ask questions of your inner voice and spontaneously to meditate is in an empty church: it is private and quiet, you will not be disturbed even if your eyes are closed, and the environment is filled with the symbols, thoughts and emotions of others who have come there before to contact their inner selves.

TRY IT!

- Make a list of contemplative places near your work or home.
- Alternatively, create a space in your home or garden to use for contemplation.
- Schedule a time each day for one week to spend in a contemplative spot you have chosen or created.
- Visit each chosen spot for one half-hour each day, for one week. How does each spot compare to the others? Does one seem more conducive to getting answers?
- If you wish, spend the first part of each day's half-hour reading one of the chapters from this book. Then close your eyes and listen.

TRY IT!

1970s best-selling author Robert Ringer reports a technique he has used successfully. He calls it Factual Meditation and employs it on his most perplexing questions. It involves sitting in a quiet room, without interruption or distraction, at a desk with nothing but a pad and pen and the question in mind. He waits until the answer comes. In the beginning, he could do it for only fifteen minutes, but, as he persisted, he was able to do it for as long as eight hours at a session. He reports many great breakthroughs, including marketing his million-seller book, *Looking Out for Number One*, by placing a full-page ad for it in the *Wall Street Journal*, which had not been done before.

TRY IT!

- Sit at a desk in a quiet room with nothing but a pad and pencil, and a question in mind.
- Wait.
- Write down any answer that comes into your mind.

TRY IT!

Marilyn Mosley, president of Laurel Springs School, an online primary and secondary school, relates:

In 1990 or 1991 I went to the Hopi Indian Reservation in Arizona and we kind of meditated together with the people there. Since that time, I've just sort of been able to, pretty much every night, just before I go to bed, I write. I just sit in bed. Oftentimes, I don't even ask a question, I just ask what the message is and I write down whatever it is that comes up, that I feel like I'm supposed to know. I think I get words more than images. I kind of get a train of thought, and I've noticed that I don't censor what I get, I just pretty much write it. Even if it seems unusual to me, or strange, I just write whatever I get. Sometimes, it's more intense than at other times. Sometimes, I feel I'm really getting something and sometimes it feels like I'm not. But, most of the time, it sort of has a life of its own. What I've noticed about the inner voice, for me, is that it isn't usually related to the day-to-day mundane level. It's not a mental process as much as it is a–kind of a spiritual process, I guess. It isn't something that I am thinking about in trying to figure things out. It simply is what comes through. It's always good. For me the inner voice is always the very highest, the best in a most profound way.

TRY IT!

- Experiment with finding the best time for you to be receptive to the inner voice:

- Just before sleep, sit up in bed with pen and pad; take a few deep breaths; allow any thoughts to come in; write down what you get.

- When you first get out of bed in the morning, find a quiet place to sit up, breathe and listen. Write out your thoughts, images or impressions.

- If going home for lunch is an option, stop there one day when the house is quiet and listen. Write down what you hear.

- Between appointments during the work day, stop into a church, sit quietly and listen. Write down any messages that come.

- Take a few moments to listen in a quiet place during one of the "dead times" in your day–waiting for dinner or any time that is spent in anticipation of a routine event. Use a pen and pad to record your thoughts.

TRY IT!

Nancy Freier, Internet publisher:

I get a form of automatic writing. It takes practice, practice, practice. Use whatever method to quiet your mind that is comfortable for you. I always start with a question in mind so when I reach that inner plane, I listen for the answer to that question. It comes to me like a whispering in my inner ear. I hear the words and then I write (or type) them out. Usually I don't hear the entire concept all at once, but am given the idea word by word. Sometimes an entire picture is revealed to me and then the angels spell it out as I am able to write it. In a sense, you could say I take dictation from the angels. I just write the words as they are spoken to me.

TRY IT!

Are you faced right now with a major decision in your life requiring some action (illness, job change, household move, relationship, finance, parenting)? What can it hurt to sit in a quiet place, take a few deep breaths, ask what to do and write down any answer that comes?

TRY IT!

Take any problem in your life and follow these steps :

INNER VOICE ACCESS STEPS:

- *Know that you are worthy to hear.*

  - *Formulate a question.*

    - *Quiet the mind.*

    - *Anticipate hearing.*

  - *Listen intently and patiently.*

- *Pay attention to whatever you get.*

  - *Write down your answer.*

CHAPTER V

Discernment

God said to Abraham: "Kill me a son."
Abe said, "God, You must be
putting me on."

Bob Dylan, "Highway 61 Revisited"

A central problem for everyone listening to the inner voice is the problem of whether it is the intellect speaking, the inner voice, or some other influence that is not in our best interest. The spectrum of this problem runs from deciding whether or not to go to the store, to whether an inner direction to lie is correct, to whether the voice you are hearing is that of a demon.

It should be clear to the listener that the inner voice is his own voice, that it is not coming from another being and that it is not merely the intellect or the egoic self speaking. But how is that accomplished? We first exclude inner voice imitations.

1. What the Inner Voice Is Not

A. The Ego Voice–Flattery or Fear

In almost thirty years of meditating and following what I got, I have only had two or three inner voice "pats on the back."

A TEACHER OF METAPHYSICS
IN CASTLETON, VIRGINIA

It is the still small voice that the soul heeds, not the deafening blasts of doom.

— WILLIAM DEAN HOWELLS

The voice of our individual ego strongly and cleverly tells us that we are truly unique, a special saint or scoundrel. In fact, the surest way to tell if you are listening to your egoic voice, and not to your inner voice, is whether the message is accompanied by either flattery or fear. The egoic voice is a voice of separation and is accompanied by judgment, good or bad: "You have been chosen," "You are very spiritual," "You have been elevated to higher dimensions than others," "You are destroying the group," "You're not getting it," "You are not worthy to have God speak to you."

The inner voice is nonjudgmental to the point of being totally impersonal, neither flattering nor deriding. Its messages are often short, to the point, completely helpful, and delivered in recognizable, but impersonal, love; and, having spoken, the inner voice moves on, without staying to chat about our good and bad characteristics.

B. The Intellect

Our intellect is like a supercomputer, running every idea through our memory banks, searching for matches to evaluate, to test against previously held views, to judge. And this supercomputer runs in parallel, chattering along: "Where did I leave the keys?" "I have to call my brother today." "What time is it?" "The tip is always double the tax." "Why can't my daughter learn algebra?"

The inner voice transcends. The inner voice sounds the same as the sound of our chattering internal monologue, but it speaks with authority: "Walk this way." "Take this job." "Hug her." The strength, clarity and brevity of the message often signals its true source.

C. The Subconscious

The inner voice is direct: "Go see Mr. Jones." "Call the vendor back." "Listen to your brother." The subconscious, however, is indirect, a land of dreams and symbols holding seemingly important messages, if we could only understand them! It is as if, as Plato says, we are looking at reality by seeing only the shadows it throws on the wall of the cave of our subconscious mind, which shows us weird shapes and fantastic designs. The inner voice reserves the right to speak to us through our subconscious, but, if we misinterpret the symbol or the dream, we have not understood the message. Ask again! The inner voice seems never to tire of answering our sincere questions, and the inner voice can be very direct when we ask again.

D. The Mass Mind

We are creatures of our culture, and it deeply affects us. We take on its meanings, values and desires, often without realizing it. Such cultural mores are not the inner voice. A high-school teacher relates:

> I was teaching a class of teenage boys recently, and one of them was being particularly obnoxious. The thought suddenly occurred to me that I should just "blow him away." I was shocked at myself: where did that come from? Upon reflection, I realized that, the day before, the boys had been talking about deer hunting and their fascination with guns and that I had just seen a particularly violent TV show. The images of violent, unilateral solutions to problems had been bombarding my subconscious mind for days. No wonder a violent solution to this student's behavior came into my mind. I am constantly reminded of the power of our unconscious influences: TV, movies, popular songs, news, books and commonly shared opinions.

2. Channeling Considered

There are more things in heaven and earth, Horatio,
Than are dreamt of in your philosophy.

HAMLET, ACT 1, SCENE 5

We leave it to the ages fully to explore the unseen world and all of its personalities, to enter that world through drugs, and to discern which paths go furthest, and which lead to insanity, addiction or harm to the traveler. We do know that forging a personal link with the inner voice results in beauty, truth and goodness in the life of the seeker.

There is one form of channeling–mediumship–that is not the inner voice. A "medium" enters an altered state of consciousness (i.e., a trance, hypnotic state, or drug-influenced condition), allows consciousness to leave his or her body and allows another, discarnate being to use that body. When the spirit being leaves the channeler's body, the channeler remembers nothing, but is exhausted, depleted. Mediumship has been exhibited throughout history and in all cultures in various ways, through differing mediums, priests, shamans, oracles and possessors.

To our discernment, such communication of information from a source outside of the self is *NOT* the inner voice. It seems easier to listen to advice from another about our most pressing problems than to develop the answers from the truth within ourselves. An old Japanese proverb says: "Give a man a fish and he eats for a day; teach a man to fish and he eats for life." And so we feel it is with establishing a conscious connection with the inner voice: the experience of finding our own inner voice to resolve life's challenges is more important than listening to a disembodied spirit tell us its experience.

Avoiding channeling is perhaps the easiest method of discernment. In the most extreme forms of channeling, the listener intentionally becomes a vehicle for another being. The voice coming through such a passive receptor is not the listener's own voice and is not an expression of the listener's own free will. Why channel? If channeling

LISTEN TO YOUR INNER VOICE

brings with it the possibility of messages from lesser-evolved beings, if channeling weakens the channeler's health, and if access to truth is as close as breathing, why channel? In other words, if you can talk to God, why accept anything less?

We seem to welcome without reservation the insights flashed to us by our own intuition, but we puzzle over channeling. Why? At the heart of every definition of channeling lies the concept that the information coming through us originates with another spirit, not ourselves. Can we trust it? Is it acting in our best interests? At the heart of the inner voice lies the concept that the spark of divinity speaking in us as our inner voice is an inherent part of ourselves connected to all of the rest of the divinity in the universe. In essence, although enhanced, connected to, and empowered by God, the inner voice is the divine part of our unique selves speaking, God's selfless gift of Self to each of us. We trust the inner voice because, like intuition, it comes solely from our own essence, not from another being.

But isn't our inner link to the divine simply another form of channeling a spirit, in this case our own Higher Self? Think of the connection between each human being and their inner voice as similar to the relationship among individual fish swimming together in a huge school. In nature, the fish in the school are perfectly aligned in purpose; they move as one body and present themselves to the visible world as one huge entity. In reality, however, no fish "controls" any other fish, tells it where to swim, or infringes on its free will. Any of the fish in the school is free at any time to leave the alignment and swim its own course without the protection of the school. So it is with the body, mind and Spirit of humankind.

3. The Voice of Love, Not Fear

And suddenly a great tempest arose in the sea, so that the boat was covered with waves. …Then His disciples came to Him and awoke Him, saying, "Lord, save us! We are perishing!" But He said to them, "Why are you fearful, O you of little faith?" Then He arose and rebuked the winds and the sea. And there was a great calm.

MATTHEW 8:24—26

Only when we step away from fear can we possibly hear the inner voice.

NEALE DONALD WALSCH

In Robert Wall Crary's, THE STILL SMALL VOICE, God says:

It is very important that you learn to distinguish between My Still Small Voice and the voice of the negative force—the voice of darkness. This negative voice can come to you from any source in the outer world or from the darkness of your own soul if you let it…. Its attributes are the opposite in every respect to those of My Voice….

The negative voice will always appeal to your lower nature, to the satisfaction or fulfillment of personal or selfish motives, desires or needs.

By the "voice of darkness" we mean a negative message in our inner monologue, a voice that creates fear or agitation, a voice that encourages us to be selfish or unkind. The inner voice is always a voice of love, not fear.

Resisting the voice of darkness can be seen in this experience related in an interview with Neale Donald Walsch, author of CONVERSATIONS WITH GOD:

My executive director called me about five weeks ago and suggested we needed to let go of somebody who works for our foundation because they weren't performing, in his point of view, their task appropriately. I asked him why he felt that way and what his recommendations were and so forth, and he laid out his whole scenario, and felt that we needed to let this person go, that was his recommendation to me, and he'd wait for my answer. I said, "Thank you very much for your input." Obviously, I sat there and I thought about that, is this the highest thought on this subject? Is this the thought that contains the greatest amount of love? Is this the thought that produces the grandest joy? The answer was clearly no. So, I called the executive director back and I said "I heard your concerns, and I hear what you're saying, and I have to tell you that that doesn't feel like the appropriate response in this situation. Let's search for another response." He said:

"I don't know what that response would be." He said: "I've thought about it a lot and I think we need to let this guy out of here." I said, "I want you to think about some other response," and he said, "I don't know what it would be." I said: "I understand that you don't, but if you thought you did, what would your answer be?" And he called me back within twenty minutes: "I know what we have to do, we need to talk to him and bring him in and help him understand that his performance is not what it should be and ask him what we could do to help." I said, "You got it, you've got it." This guy now, by the way, in the past five weeks, has turned into the most valuable employee. All he really needed was to know that he was loved, and that his work was truly valued, that he was being seen, and even perhaps, that he was watched. That somebody was caring whether he did it right or did it wrong, and that we were closely monitoring his activities to make sure that he was serving us and not just blowing it off, and whatever change took place there, in the past five weeks, this guy has turned into a model employee that we wouldn't even dream of letting go. In fact, we're giving him a raise.

Finally, consider the following expression of the way to approach the inner voice from the director of technology of a steel company:

Your own emotions play a major role in your ability accurately to use the inner voice. Any emotion but love can interfere with that direct contact. If you're worried, if you're angry, if you're confused, I don't care what the emotion is, other than love, it's a hazard on making that contact. I would say that everyone has to guard against the impact of their own personal emotions on the contact with the inner voice.

You can't contact the inner voice unless you're centered. You can't be centered unless you're in love. That's easier said than done sometimes. Now, people say they don't have any inner voice, that "I don't hear words." I believe it's primarily because of the interference of their own personal emotions. This requires the building of discipline, which comes from your meditative practice, your surrender of your attachments to the world, your commitment to the Oneness of Spirit, and the one power of God. It gradually builds and becomes solid.

For me, there was quite a period of time, over several years, when I had a practice: when I had a decision that I was asking for, that I felt my own emotions might be able to color, or interfere with, I would ask for verification in the Spirit of Truth, which is mentioned in the Bible. I could recognize that as a separate voice, and a beautiful, perfect way of validating what I believed I had received from the inner voice. Now, that passes also. You pass through that point where you have any difficulty in your confidence of the contact with the inner voice. You really are approaching the point where you are the inner voice. Your whole reality shifts. Instead of your reality being the material world, your reality is only that which is of God. Nothing else is reality, it's illusion. As that takes hold, then you're one with the inner voice without conflict or confusion.

4. Am I Crazy?

They say when you talk to God, you are praying; when He talks to you, you are schizophrenic.

LILY TOMLIN

Ignoring our inner voice is encouraged by our culture, and this takes some effort to overcome. As stated by Nancy Freier:

People seem to have a fear about voices in the head, like I once did. Every so often you hear something really negative on the news about voices—somebody heard voices in their head.

What distinguishes my listening to my inner voice from the ravings caused by mania or delirium? Each person must answer that question individually, but over time a number of general guidelines have emerged. The inner voice, in a fashion that seems to work in the best interests of men and women, is one that is loving, positive and conducive to the good of the whole. A voice that over time is not reliably for the good of the whole, that comes from a place of scarcity, fear or guilt, or that counsels harming another, is not the inner voice.

How do you tell the difference? Consider the following experience of Nancy Freier:

When I first heard an inner voice, I was very much in grief. My fiancé had just died and I didn't really care if I lived or died at the time, except that I was afraid to die. I didn't want to die, but I was almost afraid to live too. This voice that started talking to me was very comforting. It wasn't scary, which confused me, because I thought "Man, if you're losing your mind, why would it be so comforting?" In the beginning, this experience was very spontaneous. I think it was an answer to a desperate prayer that I needed help, I needed answers right then, or—or else. And, this voice came in my head and it said something like, "This is not the end; this is just the beginning." I took that to mean this is not the end of my life, but just the beginning of a new life. For me, it was pretty profound. The only prior knowledge I had about hearing a voice inside my head was that it meant you were crazy. And, when that happened to me, that's exactly what I thought. Although,

what do you compare it to? Because, you only know yourself, and when you hear this voice that isn't familiar to you . . . I thought I was crazy. In fact, I tried to check myself into a psychiatric hospital, but they didn't keep me. To this day I wish I knew who I talked to that night, because I would go back and thank him. I guess that was just the way my path needed to unfold and when I left there that night, after this doctor said that I was all right, that this was something normal from what he could tell, I was so relieved I can't even begin to tell you. Following the death of my fiancé, I wondered what else was going to happen to me.

I left there relieved, but, in the same breath, I needed to know that, if I hadn't lost my mind, then what is this voice? That moment started my search for answers. From that point forward, I met certain people—quite by accident (but there are no accidents)—who would bring me messages or pieces of the inner voice puzzle that I was trying to figure out. Actually, what developed, after reading several books and talking to others, was that this voice in my head was that of an angel.

5. How to Be Sure

I believe that God is in me as the sun is in the color and fragrance of a flower—the Light in my darkness, the Voice in my silence.

HELEN KELLER

What everyone wants to know when they first awaken to this inner voice is, "How can I be sure that this is the voice of Divine Mind?" We all seek a foolproof technique or answer to this most important question, but the universal experience is that each person's connection with Divine Mind, and with the ego, is unique. Each person devises his or her own link, as unique as fingerprints. We do know, however, that we gain confidence as we keep practicing, until there is no longer any doubt about whether Divine Mind is speaking. Each individual must personally determine whether he or she is listening to the inner voice, and perhaps that is part of the job we have on earth.

One thing is clear: any coloring of the inner voice will skew the results. So neutrality is an important element of the attitude of a person who desires to hear the inner voice. Detachment from emotional coloring of the answer is the paramount skill in listening. Be honest: Do I really prefer one alternative to the other? Would the other alternative be acceptable, even if it's not my first choice? If we have really made up our minds before we ask, there will be little the inner voice will do to influence the choice (which has really already been made). For example, if you desperately want to pursue a questionable relationship, the inner voice cannot help unless you can get to a place where pursuing and not pursuing the relationship are equally acceptable.

We are not concerned here with going against the will of Spirit–that presumes that Spirit sees us in terms of "rights" and "wrongs" instead of simply loving us–but with detouring from our path of self-realization, only to return after we have been left unfulfilled by the experience. Spirit deeply respects our free will, to the point of letting us get lost until we want to return. A retired farmer from Latrobe, Pennsylvania, puts it this way:

> When you are in Oneness, you've fallen into God's care. God does not see anyone in the human condition. He just separates from them. He sees people as in the story of the Prodigal Son, which is a beautiful story. But, all the time the Prodigal Son was blowing his inheritance and living in a human world, God just left him alone. He didn't send him any get well cards or anything. It's when the Prodigal Son turned around and said, "I've decided I've got to come home," did things begin to happen. God looks after his son/daughter. He has love beyond our conception. "All that I have is yours," but it's not that until you're one with God. You've got to be His son or daughter to have any benefit of the Holy Spirit. The only way, I believe, that you can be in attunement with that is through your inner voice.

A. Testing the Validity of the Inner Voice

Many persons adopt the technique of asking several times when in doubt about the answer. Others ask that the voice be confirmed in the Spirit of Truth (John 14:17, John 16:13). Still others ask that the intended action be blocked if the voice is misunderstood.

How to be sure of the inner voice? Test it! As stated by God in Robert Wall Crary's book *THE STILL SMALL VOICE*:

> In using the empirical, scientific method, you prove the existence of a physical law by careful experimentation, and then you accept it as a fact and put your faith in it. To prove to yourself the reality of My Spiritual Law, once I have brought it to your awareness from within you, put your full faith in it, and live within it; then My Truth substantiates your faith as My Law is fulfilled in your life.

Consider the following test of the inner voice used by Walter T. Haswell, a metallurgical engineer in Syracuse, New York :

Well, as an engineer, I developed various ways to test the inner voice, one of them being that every day I had set down a list of company stocks that I would follow, and used the inner voice to predict how they would close for each day. I took about eight stocks. I would have no other contact with the stock market before I checked next morning's newspaper. I would have written down how each stock would close from my inner voice. Lo and behold, it was not very long before I was essentially 100 percent, that I could tell where every stock was closing.

I did this strictly as an exercise. Using it for my own investments was something that I was very leery of. So, I asked my inner voice if I could use this for my investments. The answer was one of the typical kind of answers I get: "Certainly, you and I are One." Now, I've opened the door, because there is a charge involved with that, you better look carefully at how you're using it. The returns that you make using your inner voice had better be in the Spirit, or you're corrupting it.

There is a long tradition of looking for ways to be sure, to distinguish between the human mind and Divine Mind. St. Theresa of Ávila, a sixteenth-century Spanish mystic, distinguished between divinely spoken inspirations (which she called "locutions") and the workings of her own mind, as reported in *THE CRUCIBLE OF LOVE*, by E. W. Trueman Dicken:

> ... by the simple criterion that there is a difference between talking and listening .... whereas a divine locution brings peace, love and humility to the soul, a self-induced one does not. ... it is also characteristic of divine locutions that they persist in the memory with peculiar clarity, so that they are remembered with complete and literal accuracy quite indefinitely through the years. Spurious revelations on the contrary are seldom so memorable.

B. Go Higher and Ask Again

> Call to Me, and I will answer you ....
>
> JEREMIAH 33:3

Have you ever tried to read faint words on a copy of a copy of a copy of a document? Is the number a "3" or an "8"? You cannot quite see it; there is too much interference; it is too far removed from the source document; you must look at a version closer to the original. It is the same with the inner voice. If we get the vague feeling that the inner voice message is questionable, our best course of action may be to throw out the results and get closer to the original. How? Repeat the effort in an attempt to go higher in consciousness, "higher" meaning more exalted, deeper into a prayerful state, less distracted by the details of daily life, more at one with the inner voice. In other words, try harder to hear the inner voice! Jessie K. Crum, in her book THE ART OF INNER LISTENING, summarizes it this way:

> While continuing the effort to establish deeper and more meaningful contact with Higher Mind, I asked if I were making progress, and if the thoughts coming to me were really from the Higher Mind and not from lower mind. I received this answer: "You have made some progress. Your aspirations are helpful, but aspiration alone is not enough. You need to make an effort each day for contact through meditation, listening and writing. Consciousness at the human level is not a perfect receiver. The magnetic thread which connects higher and lower mind is still weak and wavering. As you perfect and train the instrument of lower mind, it will become a better reflector of Higher Mind. Write each day. This will help to strengthen the link. You are fearful that the messages you receive come from lower mind. Even though words are supplied by lower mind, the inspiration for them comes from Higher Mind. Be aware, however, that lower mind can color, shade or even distort messages, according to preconceived ideas and beliefs. This may be very slight if you strive to be impersonal and if you do not hold tenaciously to beliefs and dogmas that have colored or influenced your thinking. The lack of sureness as to the authenticity of the source will pass when the connecting band is stronger."

C. Love More: Only Divinity Gets In When Love Is Going Out

> My sheep hear My voice, and I know them, and they follow Me.
>
> JOHN 10:27

We all occasionally feel interference with our inner voice connection; we feel that something might be trying to prevent our listening to that voice. How can we remove the interference seeking to penetrate our heart? For many, the solution is to direct attention to the heart and to expand love. Think of your children, your parents, cause your love for them to pour out of your heart uncensored (and perhaps even undirected). Continue to allow love to expand in you, through you and around you, until you are love and there is no other. Only God can get through that. So much for psychic influences!

D. On Surrender Versus Technique

> The only tyrant I accept in this world is the still voice within.
>
> MAHATMA GANDHI

We have discussed discernment techniques, but these are only guidelines and may reflect our intellect's desire to control. However, the inner voice works in an opposite direction: the more surrendered (or consecrated) we are to Spirit, the more Spirit can lead and the more clearly we can hear the inner voice. Focusing on technique in listening to the inner voice is actually limiting. Focusing on surrender, as opposed to focusing on technique, is actually the best technique to discerning the inner voice.

> Sometimes . . . it may even come—as it came to myself—not by book, or picture, nor lecture, but by a voice that seemed to ring

out within me and yet without me, that was clearly not my own that, unthinking, I answered in spoken words, as though speaking to one like myself. I was in a City office, late one evening, in that strange silence of the City when all the human side has ebbed away to the suburbs, and you get that utter solitude which only this crowded City knows in the quiet hours of the evening, and in the Voice was something that seemed to me, at the moment, a little stern, clear, firm, exacting. "Are you willing to surrender everything in order that you may know the truth?" And all simply, unquestioningly, I answered: "Surely, that is all I need." But it went on, insistent: "Is there nothing that you hold back? Will you let all go?" And again the answer: "There is nothing I will not surrender if I can only know." And then the voice changed into a music, full, as it were, of smiling and benevolent compassion: "Within a very little time the Light shall arise." And

then again the silence fell, and I was left wondering what had occurred.

INITIATION: THE PERFECTING OF MAN, BY
ANNIE BESANT

Asking for Spirit's help in discernment is also effectively used by many. As stated by Patricia Jepsen Chuse:

> One of the things that we have to do if we really want to find our inner voice within ourselves and begin to walk with it, is to trust it. To build a line of trust—a real line of faith. That, for me, is where God comes in, or Christ[2], or Spirit.

2   "Christ," a word overloaded with the interpretations of millions of humans for thousands of years, means for this book not the historical Jesus but a consciousness of perfected man, which Jesus had. "He that believes in me, the works that I do shall he do also; and greater works than these shall he do." John 14:12. The Greek word "christos" literally means "anointed one" and refers to a special kind of person, but not a particular, historical person. "Christ consciousness" thus simply refers to each human's awareness of his own divinity, power and love in Spirit's eyes, be they Jew, Muslim, Buddhist, Christian, or Jesus himself.

When I am focused on Christ or God, and know that God as the Inner Voice is with me, then I'm going to step out and trust. If I don't receive something quite right, I know that the door to that action is going to be shut in my face, and I'm not going to walk the wrong way. I just give Spirit the permission to shut the door on my action if it is based on a misunderstanding of the inner voice. I don't want to get caught in phenomena.

6. Discernment By Consulting Others

The following statement from Thomas Merton suggests that one solution is to check important answers with a trusted spiritual advisor:

The most dangerous man in the world is the contemplative who is guided by nobody. He trusts his own visions. He obeys the attractions of an inner voice, but will not listen to other men. He identifies the will of God with anything that makes him feel ... [an] interior glow. And if the sheer force of his own self-confidence communicates itself to other people and gives them the impression that he really is a saint, such a man can wreck a whole city or religious order or even a nation. The world is covered with scars that have been left in its flesh by visionaries like these.

Experience counts. Asking a trusted advisor to confirm an important decision or questionable guidance has been helpful to many. Individuals with many years of experience with the inner voice are more confident and discerning. But the question arises: "Why would another person have clearer guidance about my life?" Isn't the purpose of the inner voice to experience oneness with one's higher self and to design one's own life? The danger of becoming dependent on an advisor is that of building faith in turning to the advisor rather than turning within.

Many religious orders rely on the wisdom of advisors, as with the Jesuits who assign an experienced priest to all members of the order to review their spiritual insights and internal directives.

If what we perceive to be our inner voice is counseling a course of action that is not characterized by harmlessness, we are on very dangerous ground and should ask again and again until harmlessness becomes one of the features of the counsel, if that is our guidance. However, the best we can do in life is to do what we think is right, and that includes discerning our inner voice.

Ultimately, we all must stand in our own truth. But it never hurts to check with someone either.

If you do not get it from yourself, where will you go for it?

THE GOSPEL ACCORDING TO ZEN BY ZENRUI

7. The Practical Benefits of Discernment

He who knows others is wise, but he who knows himself is enlightened.

LAO-TZU

Many persons, upon learning discernment, simply incorporate the inner voice into their daily activities. Consider the following example of Ramaa Mosley, a music video director in Hollywood, California:

I use the inner voice in my work when choosing what jobs to take. So, with my business, somebody will send me a project, in this case a music video, a song, then I'll use my inner voice to say whether I should do that job or not. There have been times where I've gotten a real strong "no" response, when I tune in to it, even though everything else looks great, especially financially. So, like the money might be really good, but I'll tune to my higher self and get the response that no, it's not the right project.

I especially do it in relationship to the people I work with. So, when I'm hiring a crew, or my producers send over assistant directors, or directors of photography for me to consider, I use my inner voice completely. I'll get a real strong response about people. I'm almost much better at reading and getting responses about people than anything else. I have an immediate sense. In fact, recently, I had to hire an assistant director, and the person they sent me, outwardly, anyone would have been concerned. This person was really funky looking and people are pretty funky in the music industry anyway, but he was really funky. When I first saw him I thought "uh oh." Then, I just tuned into myself and got the answer—the response said yes, he was the person. We hired him and it turned out to go very, very well. But, typically I probably would

have been like much more critical towards this person because of his appearance had I not checked with my inner voice.

Consider the following example from a lender liability lawyer:

I began studying the inner voice after taking up meditation as a way to deal with the stress generated by the conflict in my work. In our adversarial system, each side's job is to point out the weaknesses in the other side's case, and the theory is that, out of this dialectic, truth emerges. This puts particular emphasis on the advocate's effectiveness—and leads to stress for the advocate when the countless unforeseeable consequences of strategy decisions occur which tilt the balance of the battle in a case away from his side.

In meditation I began asking about the countless unpredictable decisions I had to make in my cases: "Which of the alternatives do I choose?" I began getting answers. As I followed them, they always seemed to work out for the best interests of all involved, including me and my clients. When I realized that this was happening, I never again made a significant case decision without checking on my inner voice, and I have never been sorry about having followed what I got. I do not know if I won more cases, but I leave the playing field every day with appropriate results and peace in my heart.

Just for an experiment, I decided once to let the inner voice do all of the work during the argument of a case before the judge. The other side got up and presented their case. My turn came and I simply waited for the inner voice to tell me what to say. I waited and waited, but nothing came. Finally, the judge said: "Counselor, do you have anything to say on behalf of your client?" I then gave my prepared argument. From this experience, I learned that I had to do my job, too.

Before my next court argument, I asked the inner voice to assist me in the argument, which I had prepared thoroughly for. The inner response I got was: "I will give you the words." When my turn came, I started the argument I had carefully prepared—and found that key words just seemed to pop out at the right time and have effects I could not have hoped for. Words had meanings in the listener's ears that had less forceful meanings in my mind; so the inner voice seemed to be at work. Expressions would pop up that I hadn't planned—like sincerely complimenting the other side's careful attention to detail on a point—that favorably disposed the judge to my side of the case. Afterwards, people came up to me and commented that there almost seemed to be a glow in the room when I spoke. After this experience, I never go to court without asking the inner voice to help me, to "give me the words."

HOW TO

Discernment

Some of the messages we receive seem perfect, while others seem questionable. Here are some methods that have helped others discern whether the messages they received were from the inner voice:

- Ask the question again, from the point of view of what's best for the whole versus what's best for me. The answer may be different, and more loving.
- Evaluate the truth of the message by its content. Are you being told to kill your son? Is harmlessness to yourself and others inherent in the message?

- Evaluate whether the message carries the feeling of joy or the feeling of negativity. Does the message embody ". . . your Highest Thought, your Clearest Word, your Grandest Feeling. Anything less is from another source. . . . The Highest thought is always that thought which contains joy. The Clearest Words are those words which contain truth. The Grandest Feeling is that feeling which you call love." *Conversations with God, Book 1*

- Ask at different times and when in different moods, to determine whether the answers are consistent.

- Ask for confirmation from the Biblical Spirit of Truth (John 14:17; John 16:13).

- Consult with an experienced inner voice listener.

- Test the inner directions you receive against objective facts or events that happen in your life.

- Reconsider whether you are totally detached from the outcome before asking again.

- Ask that Spirit block your intended action if the inner voice is misunderstood.

- Watch the doors open.

TRY IT!

A Central California couple uses this discernment method:

We often meditate together at the same time each day because we find that our meditations are stronger, or clearer, when we meditate together rather than apart. When we are both interested in getting answers on the same subject, we talk about the subject beforehand and formulate a question together. Then, we both ask the same question in our meditation. We usually get the same answer–oftentimes it is not the answer we expected–and the answer we each get is frequently phrased in virtually the same words. It has always worked out very well for us when we have followed the identical directions we have gotten, and we always do follow the identical ones. On the few occasions when we get different answers, we put the question aside–it's as if the answer is not quite ready for us yet. We have come to trust the inner voice discernment we get by each asking the same question.

TRY IT!

Suggest to your partner that you both try to seek inner guidance on the same question. When you agree upon a subject:

- Prepare pen and paper for each of you.
- Talk about the subject and what you each want to know about it.
- Formulate a one-sentence question that you both agree states the essence of what you want to know about the question. For example: "What can we do to get out of debt?" "How do we find a place to live we both love?" "What contribution can we make to better our community?"

- Sit straight in a comfortable, quiet position together in the same room.
- Close your eyes, take a few deep breaths, and focus on the joint question.
- Listen for any internal answer.
- When an answer comes write down the exact words it comes in.
- Compare what each of you has received.
- Agree to take some action on the common message you receive.
- After thirty days, review the results of the actions you have taken to see whether the inner guidance was accurate and productive of useful information on your joint question.

CHAPTER VI

Wisdom

*Behold, I stand at the door and knock.
If anyone hears My voice and opens the
door, I will come in to him and dine with
him, and he with Me.*

REVELATION 3:20

1. The Universal Voice

We have examined in prior chapters attuning to the inner voice to ask for personal guidance. As we become more familiar with this, we find that questions begin to occur to us to ask the inner voice, questions that we simply must have the answers to. We begin to ask those questions and we get answers, as usual. At some point, though, we also ask ourselves "Where are these questions coming from?" They are questions of universal application (What is the meaning of life? What is truth? Why are there beings rather than nothing?); they are perfectly formed; the questions obey all the rules of asking successful questions; the questions are frequently short; and the answers we receive are of profound universal wisdom. How did we get off on this track of asking philosophical questions? What's happening? Here's how Neale Donald Walsch, author of CONVERSATIONS WITH GOD, experiences this:

[Regarding asking questions of the inner voice], I just have to wait for this particular feeling that comes over me, which I call "the knock at the door feeling," where I'm being really invited, or urged, or it's almost impossible to ignore that feeling of needing to get up, or stop what I'm doing, whatever, and get to the yellow legal pad when that process begins. The questioning part of it works both ways. To a very large degree, I experience that both the questions and answers are being what I want to call "inspired," or given to me. By that, I mean there have been times in the dialog that I've had—which of course has turned into a trilogy of books—that questions have been asked, or given me to ask, to which I've felt I already knew the answer, or questions which did not really occur to me, I mean in my conscious mind—the questions that were given to me—and then the answer will come right after it. It's almost as if God wants the question asked so God can then give the answer. That's rather like a lawyer in the courtroom leading the witness I suppose, but I think that sometimes, there's a lot of leading the witness going on here, in this dialog, that God will give me an answer to a question, or I'll hear in my mind's ear an answer to the question and then another question will come along right behind it. Sometimes, it's a question that hadn't occurred to me, Neale, at a conscious level. Sometimes, it's a question to which I think I already know the answer, but there's a thought, apparently, at some higher level that it needs to be asked for the benefit of others.

In short, there comes a time on our inward journey when the universe seems to take an active role, to lead the way by suggesting to us universal questions that lead to profound answers, from which we learn life's lessons as the answers manifest in our lives. Why is this happening? Why do we seem to be "invited" to ask certain questions, as if we are hearing a "knock at the door"? Why do we suddenly start thinking "What is faith?" as we are putting the groceries away in the cupboard? Why is it that, as John Lennon said, "Life is what happens to us when we are busy making other plans"?

How else can Oneness show us the way to itself but by suggesting the universal questions to give us the experience and wisdom freely to accept Oneness? If we are truly listening to an inner voice, why can't that inner voice initiate the contact with us, rather than our always initiating the contact with it? Why can't the inner voice want to seek us as much as we want to seek it? Why does the mother want to talk to her child as much as the child wants the talk with the mother?

2. Seeking Wisdom

Do not seek to follow the footsteps of the men of old; seek what they sought.

MATSUO BASHO

Things begin to change as we move from personal to universal topics. The questions that begin demanding our attention are of a more universal nature, often appearing unbidden and perfectly formed in our minds. We will need paper and pen (or, better still, a tape recorder), because the answers may be extensive, and may come quickly. The answers to these questions will also have a different significance to us because they will begin to manifest in our lives.

In THE ART OF INNER LISTENING, Jessie K. Crum describes a session seeking universal wisdom:

> . . . my questions have ranged from the sublime to the trivial, and even to the ridiculous. As an example, a more weighty type of questioning concerned the nature of truth.
>
> "Is truth," I asked, "changeless and eternal? We constantly speak of truth and the need to find and know it. For what are we looking? Or is truth something that is glimpsed, but never grasped? Does one become aware of what truth is little by little, or does it come in a flash of light or an inner awakening?"
>
> Briefly I contemplated the questions I had written, and then I stopped thinking and just listened—listened as intently as if my very life depended upon hearing some far distant sound. Suddenly, answers to my questions entered the threshold of consciousness, and I recorded them in my notebook:

"If you could take knowledge, and add to it wisdom and understanding, you would begin to know something of the meaning of truth. Do not look for truth with a capital T. Search for something less elusive and of more immediate value to you. Look rather for the truth about yourself. Just how well do you know yourself, and how do you relate to other individuals? They, like you, have problems, fears, anxieties, frustrations, hopes, joys, and longings for completeness. You wish for understanding to discover truth? Then, be aware that self-knowledge is the beginning of understanding. Without understanding how can you expect to find truth? Many people in a vague way are looking for truth. They dream, also, of some day doing good in the world. Such ideas for most individuals are unformulated and tenuous, slumbering in hidden recesses of the mind. These dimly perceived longings may be expressed by wishing for money or time to use in helping people. Such wishful thoughts are of no more use than evanescent dreams. To help others you must first have sufficient understanding to help yourself. If you can help yourself, if you can understand yourself, then you will be ready to help those who may need your help, and who perchance may accept the help offered."

A. Formally Identify the Question

Isolate and inspect the question that's been on your mind. What is it, exactly? Ellen, for example, went through a period when she realized that she had been going through her normal daily activities with a vague thought on the edge of her consciousness, something about virtue. As the days progressed, Ellen realized that she felt somehow compelled to understand virtue more. At first, her mind wandered passively around the issue:

> I wonder if I'm virtuous. Mom acted virtuous but was it just a habit? Is virtue some sort of conditioning? What are virtues anyway? Let's see: truth, beauty... oh, is beauty a virtue? Or just something that is?

When she realized that her mind was leading her down its chattering, wandering path, she paused to think about exactly what it was she wanted to know about virtue.

B. Write the Question Down

She put her mind to work actively. "What do I want to know about virtue? I guess I want to know what virtue is." When she had that thought, "What is virtue?" popped into her mind. She wrote that question at the top of a page of paper. (Ellen keeps writing materials, or a tape recorder, handy because the answer to such a question may pour out and be lost if not captured immediately.)

C. Quiet the Mind

She then closed her eyes, quieted her mind, breathed slowly and asked: "What is virtue?"

D. Record the Answer

After a while, she heard a gentle, quiet almost faint sound of her own voice in her own mind, a "still small voice." She simply wrote down what came, even when, to her conscious mind, the answer at first seemed insignificant or too simple or not correct. In this exercise, Ellen's still small voice answered: "Virtue is My way of being. It is purity in action."

She wrote that answer down. The first question her intellect asked was, "Wasn't that just your own thought?

What makes you think that was divine?" She suspended judgment, waiting until after the exercise was complete. Upon reflection, "purity in action" did indeed seem to be a profound way of fully answering the question, "What is virtue?"

E. Results

One essential element of this process of using the inner voice to access wisdom is that after the answer comes, then that answer manifests in your life, changing it. Once the truth of the answer becomes known to you, that truth works in all of your activities relating to that concept. For example, if the answer to the question "What is virtue" is "purity in action," then you know that you're virtuous, if you are purity in action. This simple knowledge affects the way you live. And with the knowledge comes the responsibility to live your life in accordance with that principle. In Ellen's case, "virtue" had had an almost negative connotation, like the iron rules of a religion, something for an adolescent to rebel against. If the idea of virtue was that it meant being pure in action, it meant being purely who you were and acting accordingly, without guilt, apology or pretense. Ellen was free to be purely herself, which changed her consciousness and profoundly affected her behavior.

In the movie *JUMANJI*, children find a strange, old board game with unusual properties: when the dice are rolled, a message appears, and the message then manifests as a reality in the lives of the players. This is what happens when the wisdom aspect of the inner voice is accessed.

In Ellen's case, the answer came, and the question "What is virtue?" never reappeared in her mind. But in her daily life, she now knows that "purity in action" is the hallmark of virtuous conduct.

F. Where to Place Your Consciousness

The experience of seeking wisdom is more easily understood and accessed by some persons if they can work with the concept of "inner geography." In Chapter IV we looked at this idea. People's experiences vary of where to place their consciousness when seeking universal wisdom. Jessie K. Crum just listens intently; Neale Donald Walsch is inspired with a question, without meditating at all; one spiritual teacher, Patricia Jepsen Chuse, finds her consciousness works best when located in a specific place in her body:

I first experienced the inner voice as something like a higher frequency of my own mind. There were aspects of it that surprised me. For example, science and poetry, as well as new religious thought, began to pour through me. Then, as I began to focus on my third eye (the center between the eyebrows), I discovered I could consciously call in the inner voice. As I focused my attention there, I experienced wonderful feelings of completion, of fusion, and of brilliance. I was thinking with the Universe. There was such a sense of creativity, and I felt whole, rather than a small child being led by the Universe. I moved from a limited dimension of mind to a much more expanded dimension of reality. My thinking changed dramatically: essentially, I became more universal in my outlook. Due to my alignment with the inner voice, I felt that I became a citizen of the Universe. That's exciting!

This connection to the Higher Mind can only

come when we acknowledge that give and take with Spirit expression, that actual surrender into a new life. Some people don't like the word "surrender" but I think it is the best word to describe the process. To find that inner voice and to fuse with it, it is necessary to release our desires and our ideas into Spirit for, perhaps, a better design for our lives. When we can do that, we are getting closer to the function of the Spirit in us as higher intelligence, which I know as the inner voice. When we touch this place of spiritual dimension we are brilliant, we are genius. My dream is to offer a university and a vibrational space, in a creative environment, so that people can really experience this exciting new place that they have within themselves.

G. Wisdom Has Many Ways to Reach Us

The inner voice follows its own path to communicate wisdom to each individual. Consider the following example from the experience of a products liability attorney:

> For some time I had been pondering the question of what my purpose in life was, what I should be doing with the life I had been given. Following a suggestion I had read somewhere, I posed the question, "What is my divine purpose?" to my mind just before going to sleep, several nights in a row. Finally, I had a dream. In the dream, I stopped to talk with a construction worker inside the first floor of a poorly lit, dirt-floored building under construction. He was operating a piece of heavy equipment and deftly and easily moving an impossibly huge pipe shaped like a boat (submarine?) and filled with some construction material (dirt?) into position with a crane. He motioned for me to go outside, and, once we were outside, he simply said:

"Intention implies fulfillment."

When I awoke, I realized that what I had been told directly in the dream was really quite profound: we are creative beings; we are given the tools to accomplish any result we can imagine; we could not have imagined any result if we had not also been given the power to accomplish that result; and our part in the whole process is simply to form and express the intention for the results to happen.

Although I had asked a personal question, I had gotten a universal answer. My divine purpose in life was thus anything (and everything, since my purpose was not simply to work on creating just one result) I could imagine, anything that "popped into my head," anything that my inner voice suggested. I felt assured that I could actually accomplish whatever purpose came to me in that way, like the famous Walt Disney remark: "If you can dream it, you can do it."

3. Truth, Being Universal, Is in Each of Us

> "Beauty is truth, truth beauty"—that is all
> Ye know on earth, and all ye need to know.
> "ODE ON A GRECIAN URN" BY JOHN KEATS,

How do we recognize wisdom when we come upon it? Why do we know that something is profound? Why are great symphonies, paintings and other works of art recognized by everyone as great? It is so because any lofty expression of universal realities that moves people century after century resonates with the beauty, truth and goodness within each of us. If we did not all have that beauty, truth and goodness within us, we would not be able to exclaim: "Yes, that's beauty. I know it!" The universal wisdom represented by great art is recognizable by each of us.

Who can honestly doubt the beauty,

truth and goodness of the following lines from Shakespeare?

> The quality of mercy is not strain'd,
> It droppeth as the gentle rain from heaven
> Upon the place beneath. It is twice blest:
> It blesseth him that gives and him that takes.
> 'Tis mightiest in the mightiest: it becomes
> The throned monarch better than his crown;
> His sceptre shows the force of temporal power,
> The attribute to awe and majesty,
> Wherein doth sit the dread and fear of kings;
> But mercy is above this sceptred sway,
> It is enthroned in the hearts of kings,
> It is an attribute to God himself;
> And earthly power doth then show likest God's,
> When mercy seasons justice.

THE MERCHANT OF VENICE, ACT 4, SCENE 1

Or in the Gettysburg address:

Fourscore and seven years ago, our fathers brought forth upon this continent a new Nation, conceived in Liberty, and dedicated to the proposition that all men are created equal. Now we are engaged in a great Civil War, testing whether that Nation, or any nation so conceived and so dedicated, can long endure. We are met on a great battlefield of that war. We have come to dedicate a portion of that field as a final resting-place of those who here gave their lives that that Nation might live. It is altogether fitting and proper that we should do this. But, in a larger sense we cannot dedicate, we cannot consecrate, we cannot hallow this ground. The brave men, living and dead, who struggled here, have consecrated it far above our power to add or detract. The world will little note, nor long remember, what we say here, but it can never forget what they did here. It is for us, the living, rather to be dedicated here to the unfinished work they have thus far so nobly advanced. It is rather for us to be here dedicated to the great task remaining before us, that from these honored dead, we take increased devotion to that cause for which they here gave the last full measure of devotion; that we here resolve that the dead shall not have died in vain, that this Nation, under God, shall have a new birth of freedom; and that government of the People, by the People, and for the People, shall not perish from the earth.

Or in this prayer:

O Lord, make me an instrument of your Peace.
Where there is hatred, let me sow Love;
Where there is injury, Pardon.
Where there is discord, Unity.
Where there is doubt, Faith.
Where there is error, Truth.
Where there is despair, Hope.
Where there is sadness, Joy.
Where there is darkness, Light;
O Divine Master,
Grant that I may not so much
Seek to be consoled, as to console,
To be understood, as to understand;
To be loved, as to love;
For it is in giving that we receive,
It is in pardoning, that we are pardoned,
It is in dying, that we are born to Eternal Life.

ST. FRANCIS OF ASSISI

All of us recognize the wisdom in these lines because the beauty, truth and goodness contained in these lines resonates with the beauty, truth and goodness resident within all of us.

Not only do we have the capacity to recognize wisdom, but we also have the power to let it come through us, to allow the inner voice to initiate the contact with us, to create, as in the following:

> ... [A Course in Miracles] was dictated by a clear inner voice to Helen Cohen Schucman, a psychologist at Presbyterian Hospital in New York and an assistant professor of psychology at Columbia University's College of Physicians and Surgeons. Schucman ... [at the time] an atheist ... kept hearing a silent inner voice, which she called simply the "Voice." She feared she was going insane.... In September 1965 she felt she was about to begin something very unusual. A month later the Voice began dictating the Course with the opening words, "This is a course in miracles. Please take notes."

> HARPER'S ENCYCLOPEDIA OF MYSTICAL AND
> PARANORMAL EXPERIENCE

As the relationship develops with our inner voice, we each have the freedom to pursue the relationship and even to allow the inner voice to take the initiative in communicating its infinite wisdom to us. Consider the following description of such a relationship with the inner voice of Patricia Jepsen Chuse:

> Everyone has an inner voice. It is there within each one. In the words of the Bible: "Seek and ye shall find." It is connected to your higher intelligence, to your relationship and communication with God.
> It really leads you to who you are and leads you to yourself. It's a wonderful, wonderful line of energy to have with you. With that inner voice, there is nothing that you cannot accomplish; you can go for ideas and scientific discoveries that the mind of man hasn't even dreamed we could discover and accomplish. It's all there. The map of the heavens.
> The way to access it is to understand and keep asking the inner voice. For me, to access

it is through Christ in the heart. It's that absolute turning your life over to the Spirit of God, within your heart. When you do that, then you listen, and Higher Mind talks to you as divine intelligence, as the light of God. Be patient. When you make a mistake with it, don't belabor it. Find out what the mistake is and try not to make it again.

4. The Prophetic Voice

There is a special class of persons to whom the inner voice comes and initiates a special kind of communication: we call them prophets. To them, the inner voice conveys an entire flow of inspired wisdom about unknowable subjects, such as significant events in the future affecting large groups of people. Prophets have existed in all cultures and ages, from the Old Testament (it has been said that eighteen of its thirty-nine books were written by prophets), through Nostradamus (whose revelations came to him through "the subtle spirit of fire" and were accompanied by a voice, the "Divine Presence"); Mohammed, the founder of Islam; Rasputin; Joseph Smith, the founder of the Mormon religion; Edgar Cayce; Jeanne Dixon and many others. The prophet does not choose his calling: he is chosen. The inner voice initiates the contact. The tradition of prophecy has been that it is a special calling requiring serious purification and preparation, probably because of the responsibility attendant upon the effect prophecy has on large groups of people.

This is how the nineteenth-century Russian poet Alexander Pushkin put it in his poem "The Prophet" (translated by Babette Deutsch and Avrahm Yarmolinsky):

I dragged my flesh through desert gloom,
Tormented by the spirit's yearning,
And saw a six-winged Seraph[3] loom
Upon the footpath's barren turning.
And as a dream in slumber lies
So light his finger on my eyes,
My wizard eyes grew wide and wary:
An eagle's, startled from her eyrie.
He touched my ears, and lo! a sea
Of storming voices burst on me.
I heard the whirling heavens' tremor,
The angels' flight and soaring sweep,
The sea-snakes coiling in the deep,
The sap the vine's green tendrils carry.
And to my lips the Seraph clung
And tore from me my sinful tongue,
My cunning tongue and idle-worded;
The subtle serpent's sting he set
Between my lips–his hand was wet,
His bloody hand my mouth begirded.

And with a sword he cleft my breast
And took the heart with terror turning,
And in my gaping bosom pressed
A coal that throbbed there, black and
burning.[4]
Upon the wastes, a lifeless clod,
I lay, and heard the voice of God:
"Arise, oh prophet, watch and hearken
And with my Will thy soul engird,
Through lands that dim and seas that
darken
Burn thou men's hearts with this, my
Word."

As the poem expresses, God may
choose an inward traveler to speak for
Him. First, it is necessary to cleanse the
prophet candidate and for the prophet to
be completely open to, or to be surren-

3   Seraph, the celestial beings surrounding the throne of God
    and acting as messengers.

4   A burning coal. The reference is to the story of the prophet
    Isaiah, whose lips were cleansed by God with a burning coal
    to prepare him for his prophetic mission (Isaiah 6:1).

dered to, the unified vision of God in order for the "Word" to be heard: not a comfortable experience, as the Pushkin images indicate. The prophet hears the inner voice, sees the Oneness and is charged with the task of communicating the wisdom he has heard to men's hearts.

Here is the story of Isaiah from the Bible (Isaiah 6:5—9):

"Woe is me, for I am undone!
Because I am a man of unclean lips,
And I dwell in the midst of a people of
unclean lips;
For my eyes have seen the King,
The Lord of hosts."
Then one of the seraphim flew to me, having
in his hand a live coal which he had taken with
the tongs from the altar.
And he touched my mouth with it, and said:
"Behold, this has touched your lips;
Your iniquity is taken away,
And your sin purged."
Also I heard the voice of the Lord, saying:
"Whom shall I send,
And who will go for Us?"
Then I said, "Here am I! Send me."
And He said: "Go, and tell this people ...."

Why does God use prophets? Historically, prophets seem to be given revelations to communicate to the people to move them collectively forward in mankind's spiritual journey. That's why prophecy is uncomfortable for the prophet: he is chosen to present new ideas about God and the future to a complacent populace. No wonder that he must be prepared and that the journey can be difficult! How else, though, can God, completely respecting our free will, prepare the way in men's minds for new spiritual consciousness, even for the acceptance of our Oneness?

Revelation is a word from God regarding the vision and direction God wills for his people.

THE PROPHET'S REWARD
BY GREGORY WARK

The prophet John describes his experience in the Bible:

And there, on the Lord's day, I fell into a trance, and heard behind me a voice, loud as the call of a trumpet, which said: "I am the Alpha and the Omega, the First and the Last, and write down all that thou seest and send it to the seven churches in Asia ...." So I turned to see what voice it was that was speaking to me.

REVELATION 1:11—12

I will pour out my spirit upon all flesh; and your sons and your daughters shall prophesy; your old men shall dream dreams, your young men shall see visions. JOEL 2:28

But, if we are all connected to the inner voice, why are there prophets at all? Why do we have to listen to others' interpretations of the inner messages? One of the beauties of this universe is that all of its creations are unique; no two creatures are the same. Like instruments in an orchestra, the notes of the inner voice coming through each individual person contribute to the grand symphony of the spheres. Prophets may be the kettle drums of the universe.

As the Bible puts it:

Pursue love, and desire spiritual gifts, but especially that you may prophesy... he who prophesies speaks edification, and exhortation, and comfort to men.

I CORINTHIANS 14:1

5. The Word

Why do we all respond to the sound of

words? Poetry draws much of its appeal from the sound of the words. What is a song but words set to vibration? A good song "feels" good. Great orators seem to move people not only through the content of their words but also through some energy that seems to accompany the timing, pace and speaking of the words. Spiritually-minded people have often noted the power of sound:

All religious scriptures mention the Sound Current or the "Word", but unfortunately their followers are unaware of it. Hindus call it "Anahat Shabd" (unstruck music); "Akash Bani" (the celestial voice); or "Shruti" (which can be heard). Chandogya and Mandok Upanishads name it "Udgith." Nad Bind Upanshad also refers to the practice of the "Word." In Sikh scriptures, this has been expressed by the terms "Nam" (name); "Dhun" (tune); "Sach" (truth); "Anahad Shabd" (ceaseless eternal Sound); "Bani" (Word); "Gur Bani" (Guru's Word); "Shabd" (sound), etc. Mohammedans call it "Kalma" (Word); "Kalam-i-Ilahi" (voice of God); "Nada-i-Asmani" (heavenly sound); "Isme-i-Azam" (great name); or Sultan-ul-Azkar. Greek mystics refer to it as "Logos." Socrates speaks of an inner sound which transported him to realms transcendent and divine. Zoroaster speaks of it as "Sraosha." Theosophists enumerate some of the sounds that are heard within and call them "The pure white music." It is "The wind that bloweth where it listeth." . . . . "A sound is vibrating in the whole of creation. When you open your inner ear you will hear a continuous Sound (Word), which will lead you across all limitations of mind and matter. . . ."

THE INNER VOICE BY C. W. SANDERS

The Bible describes sound as follows:

In the beginning was the Word, and the Word was with God, and the Word was God. He was in the beginning with God. All things were made through Him, and without Him nothing was made that was made.
In Him was life, and the life was the light of men. And the light shines in the darkness, and the darkness did not comprehend it.

JOHN 1:1—5

What is the sound or "Word" referred to in these passages? We suggest that the vibration accompanying the Word carries the frequency and power of God, and creates. It is God's power declaring itself into manifestation. "We are to meet our Creator through the Sound Current, which keeps creation in being." (*THE INNER VOICE* by C. W. Sanders)

Modern theories of physics suggest exactly the same thing:

According to string theory, the fundamental building blocks of the universe are not particles or forces but tiny loops that vibrate in ten dimensions. Just as a four-string violin creates symphonies of sound, the harmonics of these higher dimensional strings create everything in the universe.

COLUMN ONE:
A CAREER BOLDLY TIED BY STRINGS
(LOS ANGELES TIMES, FEBRUARY 4, 1997, K.C. COLES)

6. Speaking the Word

Have you ever witnessed a preacher get up, deliver a sermon and ignite his audience with the rhythm, flow and power of a speech that seemed to have a lasting effect on your life and the lives of many others? John F. Kennedy's "Ich bin ein Berliner" speech and Martin Luther King's "I have a dream" speech were two such speeches. The experience is electrifying: it is almost as if we shift into another dimension. The words have the ring of truth. We say that such speakers have charisma, and even their printed words, long after the speech is over, like the Gettysburg address, transport us, uplifted and unified, to a higher way of thinking.

A. The Word IN Us

When we speak the Word, a progression in inner voice alignment occurs. The Word when spoken is not *TO* us but rather *IN* us. Susan G. Shumsky, in her book *DIVINE REVELATION*, discusses ways of expressing divine revelation, including "speaking-through," which "is a direct link with Spirit without going through the filter of your mind. You are lifted to the divine level, become fully identified with Spirit and speak from that place. "I and my Father are one."

As was said in *OBJECTIFICATION*, by Minerva: "Man being God's expression expresses God by expressing."

This aspect of the inner voice has a compelling active component to it–it feels as if it is sometimes necessary to speak out loud as part of the inner voice, as if the communication initiated by the inner voice must manifest itself. This speaking is speaking as the Creator, and you can feel the difference. Such "speaking" can take many forms–speaking, writing, dancing, even singing, as in the following example from the experience of a young woman:

> I was out hiking with five of my friends and camping out. We all went up to this remote peak. It was really beautiful. Suddenly, I began to experience a whole different reality and was able to connect to this incredible force, this feeling. I looked

out across the landscape and saw everything in it, the boulders, the rocks, everything. It could almost be perceived as a cliché, like everything was warping. But more than anything, I had a sense of this God energy and myself being in union. It was outrageous, I had never experienced anything like that. It was very exciting. I've had really outrageous experiences before, experiences where I went out of my body, but I hadn't had an experience like this where I felt like I had just exploded with the universe. It was really great. I felt oneness with the universe, and with my past. I had a complete connection with myself on the time track of my lifetime. So, one moment, I completely flashed to being six years old and having all these experiences, and the next moment I would be in a different time. I was incredibly connected to my childhood, because it blew away all the boundaries of time.

I started singing, as if I was singing from a God energy, with incredible power. Everyone started to sing with me. For a moment, it was like six people that were huddled around with their heads brushed up against each other, singing, and it was like our beings were just resonating. We were just singing sounds, not words or something we had heard before. The sounds had the feeling of just incredible clarity and peace. When it was done, two people came up to me and said: "When you started singing, I felt my whole body start to vibrate. Your voice was making my body vibrate." It was really incredible. I think that I was singing from a higher power, and that it was so true and potent because it was coming from that place.

B. The Effect on Those Around Us

When speaking the Word, an energy accompanies the voice and is attractive to those around, whether they are attuned to their own inner voice or not. It is instructive, dynamic, and speaks to the particular moment where the speaker is in society, in history. The Word itself, the vibration, emanates forth and is felt. Many have noticed that even the animals respond to it, that dogs and cats come closer when one is speaking the Word. Why have the great orators in history–Cicero, Patrick Henry, William Jennings Bryan–had such an electrifying effect on their listeners while giving flawless, yet extemporaneous, speeches? The Word at work. Legislators, trial lawyers, teachers, salesmen and preachers–all whose business is speaking–have had those times when beautiful oratory seemed to pour out, perfectly formed, from some inner place.

C. Speaking the Word is Creative

Then God said, "Let there be light"; and there was light. GENESIS 1:3

In *THE PROPHETIC VOICE*, Kim Clement describes the creative aspect of the Word as follows:

> The Voice of God is the source of all life. Through God's spoken word, all things that exist came into being. The earth and all that is in it is held in its place because of the power of God's spoken word. "In the beginning was the Word ...." As Paul said (Hebrews 11:3),
>
>> "By faith we understand that the worlds were framed by the word of God so that the things which are seen were not made of things which are visible."
>
> God's very expression is creative power. When He speaks, life is the result. The words carry creative power and create when spoken.

Man, created in God's image, also possesses the creative power exercisable through the spoken word. And we can all perform creation: miracle workers and people going to day jobs are separated only by their thinking about the creative power of their own spoken words. As expressed by Alice Bailey in her book *Initiation, Human and Solar*:

> Every word, differentiated or synthesized affects ... the form-building aspects of manifestation. No sound is ever made without producing a corresponding response in deva substance and driving multitudes of tiny lives to take specific forms.

The Word creates. It is the reason why affirmations ("I like myself." "I easily do the math problem." "I can resolve this disagreement." "I build cathedrals.") work to create the desired results. "I can't afford it" ensures that we will not have "it." In *The Secret Life of Plants*, by Peter Tompkins and Christopher Bird, Cleve Backster scientifically demonstrates the healing effect speaking to plants has on their health.

7. Sharing the Bounty

If you hadn't noticed yet, when wisdom is received, often it is accompanied by a request to share, as we noted in the Revelation of John and *A Course in Miracles*. Wisdom is not meant to be given as little personal jewels but to be written and printed, or at least spoken, publicly at appropriate times. It is universal truth, for the good of the whole.

And yet, it is Oneness, not wisdom, that is the goal of the inner voice, for even wisdom fades in time:

> Then I turned myself to consider wisdom and madness and folly;
> For what can the man do who succeeds the king?—Only what he has already done. Then I

saw that wisdom excels folly as light excels darkness. The wise man's eyes are in his head, but the fool walks in darkness. Yet I myself perceived that the same event happens to them all. So I said in my heart, "As it happens to the fool, it also happens to me, and why was I then more wise?" Then I said in my heart, "This also is vanity. For there is no more remembrance of the wise than of the fool forever, since all that now is will be forgotten in the days to come. And how does a wise man die? As the fool!"

ECCLESIASTES 2:12—16

HOW TO

Wisdom

To access the inner voice, we ask and listen. To access wisdom through the inner voice, it becomes necessary for us to move in consciousness to where wisdom resides, to feel the place of wisdom in our consciousness.

We may use deep space as a metaphor for consciousness. The area of wisdom for the subject we are concerned with is out there in our "deep space." We travel there by going further or deeper into a meditative state. We do that by holding firmly onto the subject. That is our compass. As we deepen our meditation, holding our focus on the subject draws us to the place of wisdom for that subject. In other words, if we ask "What is virtue?", focusing on virtue will draw us to that place of wisdom on the subject of virtue, and we will get our answer. If we deepen our meditative state and keep our mind on the subject, we unerringly direct our thoughts, like a heat-seeking missile, to the wisdom destination. We state overleaf how we access that wisdom.

TRY IT!

- Has there been a vague curiosity about something on your mind ("What is the purpose of life?" "Why do living things die?" "What does it all mean?"). See if you can identify clearly what you are curious about.

- Prepare a pen and paper, or tape recorder. Get comfortable and quiet.

- Focus on the subject. If your mind wanders, gently bring it back to the question at hand.

- Begin to write at the slightest stirring of an answer.

TRY IT!

Some of the most profound truths can be so simply stated that pearls of wisdom seem obvious, as if they were not important (e.g., "The light of the world is within you." "In separation, all is One." "All is well." "Awaken the light within." "Release My love within your heart."). This is why writing down what you get is so important. The following approach has worked for many:

- Keep a diary every day for two weeks.
- Once in a meditative state, just write whatever comes into your thoughts.
- Are you surprised at anything you have written?
- Have you stated any questions that seem to be on your mind? Are some of your writings profound?
- Highlight the writings that seem to contain wisdom with a marker and ponder them further. What do you get? Does it help in your life?
- Can you think of a way to share the wisdom you have received? In a message to a friend? In speaking to a child?

CHAPTER VII

Oneness

I and My Father are one.

JOHN 10:30

Our deepest yearning is for union. We seek union with lovers, with nature, with our own integrated selves–but ultimately this yearning returns us to union with God or Universal Mind, or the Life Force in all things.

But how is Oneness experienced? Can anyone have the experience of Oneness? We all have glimmerings of Oneness from time to time. Many can experience Oneness in nature, as in the camping example from the previous chapter. Others find Oneness in their highest meditative state. Throughout history, persons arriving at their most prayerful state have found Oneness. What does it feel like, Oneness in your most prayerful state?

- There is no conflict.
- There are no other beings.
- There is no limit on space; your mind can roam to any subject.
- There is no limit on or awareness of time.
- Your consciousness can expand and expand to any distance, length, inquiry or thought without limitation; everything is available.
- There is nothing else present but your consciousness, and you are conscious of all that is.
- You have the feeling that you are a consciousness complete.
- Essentially, everything is there, nothing is there, you are all that there is–that's Oneness.

1. The Difference Between Wisdom and Oneness

Whereas before, using the inner voice allowed us to receive wisdom from God, standing in Oneness allows us to be at one with wisdom as if we were God, which in fact we are. In wisdom, our inner voice aligns itself with Spirit's Will: "Thy will, not mine, be done." In Oneness, or union, we say: "Thy will and mine are One." Oneness is but the culmination of all we have learned about the inner voice, beginning with intuition, creativity and conscience. In the words of Neale Donald Walsch, author of CONVERSATIONS WITH GOD, "When we come to earth we forget who we are so that we can experientially appreciate Who We Are."

When we first consider the idea that we are part of God, it is often a frightening thought. However, frightening or not, if it is true, we cannot deny it and must accept this part of our selves. This possibility was eloquently stated by Nelson Mandela in his acceptance speech for his historic election as president of South Africa:

Our deepest fear is not that we are inadequate. Our deepest fear is that we are powerful beyond measure. It is our light, not our darkness, that most frightens us. We ask ourselves, who am I to be brilliant, gorgeous, talented and fabulous? Actually, who are you not to be? You are a child of God. Your playing small doesn't serve the world. There's nothing enlightened about shrinking so that other people won't feel insecure around you. We were born to make manifest the glory of God that is within us. It's not just in some of us; it's in everyone. And as we let our own light shine, we unconsciously give other people permission to do the same. As we are liberated from our own fear, our presence automatically liberates others.

Nevertheless, the creation is not the Creator. "Oneness" means that we are like individual leaves on a tree: all different, but all part of One. In the words of the Bible (John 15:5):

> "I AM the vine, you are the branches. He that abides in Me, and I in him, the same brings forth much fruit, for without Me you can do nothing."

2. The Mystical Experience of Oneness

> [Everything] is hitched to everything else in the universe.
>
> JOHN MUIR

Mysticism is a much misinterpreted word, with as many meanings as it has adherents. It is defined, in the Merriam-Webster dictionary, as:

> Mysticism: 1. The experience of mystical union or direct communion with ultimate reality reported by mystics. 2. The belief that direct knowledge of God, spiritual truth, or ultimate reality can be attained through subjective experience (as intuition or insight).

It is defined in *HARPER'S ENCYCLOPEDIA OF MYSTICAL AND PARANORMAL EXPERIENCE* as:

> The belief in or pursuit of unification with the One or some other principle; the immediate consciousness of God; or the direct experience of religious truth.

We all have the ability to experience mystical events; they are not the exclusive property of holy men fasting in caves in the Himalayas. Most ordinary people have a mystical experience at least once in their lifetimes, and we have all felt the tug of oneness in times of natural disaster. What follows is a selection of mystical experiences of regular people.

Consider the following from Virginia Sky, choreographer:

I befriended this psychic, we would do readings together. One time, she was doing automatic writing, and she called me up and said, "You need to follow the white light, the Christ light," and I said, "What is the white light?" I wasn't into metaphysics then. I didn't have any books in my home, I was always choreographing. She said, "Well, I don't know," and I said, "Is that like those ministers on TV?" She said, "No, that's just what came through." I went to bed that night, and I said the Lord's Prayer, and then almost, half cocky, I said, "Okay, bring me the white light." I couldn't sleep that night. I tossed and turned and I had a German Shepherd who was on the floor, and I just couldn't sleep, and I hate it when I can't sleep. So, I looked at my digital clock and it was 3:33.

I put my face in the pillow, which is not very comfortable, and I started to lift up, and, all of a sudden, I felt a hand push my head back in. I thought, "Oh God, who's here?" At which point, my whole apartment was flooded with white light. I felt an awe, and then a triangle appeared to my brain, and pulled away, and then the number "3" came, then the letter J, and then that disappeared, and then the letter F, and that disappeared, and then I lifted off the bed.[5] I remember looking down at myself, then I shot up through the roof and I kept thinking this is really going to hurt my head, I mean I was so literal. I looked at all the cosmos and it was so incredible. I felt like I was touched by God. Then, I came right back into the bed and I went, "Oh my God, what was that?"

I then looked again at the digital clock and it was still 3:33. I couldn't believe that this big thing happened in the blink of an eye. I thought my dog would be awake, but she

---

5   I interpreted these symbols later to mean all one, but also separate: "3" or the triangle–the Trinity or Holy Spirit; "J"–Jesus; "F"–Father.

slept through the whole thing. I thought, "I've got to call someone." Well, I couldn't call anybody at that time, so I waited until 7:00 in the morning, and I called my friend and I said, "This thing happened." She said, "That's the white light."

Or consider the following from Michael Toms:

I was deep in a depression caused by a trauma—I was about to get married and the whole thing crashed. It happened a few days before the wedding and my entire life, as I thought, just crumbled beneath me and I went into a deep and dark depression. I found myself writing and not getting a lot of sleep. I wasn't eating very well. I was sleep deprived; I was food deprived; I was spending a lot of time just writing. The writing was taking the form of letters to my former fiancé but they really were something else—I was pouring my own anxiety on paper. I was exploring my inner depths.

At some point in that process, I broke through. The breakthrough was an experience of something emerging, a real vision that everything which had happened to that point in time was for a reason. This was the turning point for me. It was my call and I had to heed it. It certainly is comparable to what I've read about as mystical experience. It was beyond what the rational mind can imagine could happen. It certainly was beyond my imagination to comprehend how it could happen, but happen it did. I had the experience in a moment of realizing the reasons for every single thing in my life and the room became filled with light. It turned into a very positive thing and it clearly was a breakthrough, turning my life in a whole new direction.

I stopped writing at that point. It was night, about 4:00 a.m. in the morning. The stars from a dark night (the moon wasn't out), you could see all the stars; it's a gorgeous night; and I just find myself crying and connecting with the Christ energy, a deep and profound experience of the Christ. Paradoxically, out of that experience, I wound up coming in touch with the spiritual philosophy of Buddhism and Taoism in a very deep way. The experience dramatically altered my life and gave me another sense. It was like reading the Bible for the first time. I received a whole new vision of Jesus and what Christianity was about. It revitalized me and gave me a radically different view of my own religion. I was raised a Catholic and I had left the church really, but this experience gave me a new appreciation of my spiritual roots. Anyway, as I said, it moved my life in a completely new direction. Out of that, eventually, I came to create New Dimensions, the work I do in the world.

Or consider the following from Jack Hart:

I have had the experience of feeling oneness many times. It seems like probably the most constant experience in my life, but, for me, it's not a union with God, but a oneness with life. The divine oneness is everywhere. It's just a constant experience. It can be in very mundane things. So often in nature you experience a certain thing where you can bring out phenomena: you're standing across from a mountain, you see the mountain breathe; you're standing on a ridge, you look down, and you see the rocks and snow move as they would over a two-thousand-year period; you walk through a forest, you're aware of every single leaf in that forest, as if you were looking at each leaf individually. You can hear the leaves, you can hear the life, you can feel things going up through them.

A Benedictine nun had the opportunity to take a sabbatical, after a lifetime of teaching, counseling, and communicating with students. She chose the austere and starkly beautiful Christ in the Desert monastery near Taos, New Mexico, and had this experience:

> I walked out into the desert one morning with only a snake stick and a little water. Taking my bearings as I moved across the desert, I began to experience a living participation in the whole of reality. In this sharply focused environment of total silence, I felt like I was one with all life; I found that I was blessing everything. This unforgettable experience, difficult as it is to capture in words, seemed to be a freeing of me from any barriers to Oneness. I felt that was a "given" experience, not something I could take steps to re-create another time.

Another experience of Walter T. Haswell, a metallurgical engineer in Syracuse, New York:

> About sixteen years ago, I had an experience where I was simply overcome by Spirit. I was meditating out on the patio, on the back of the house. It was a beautiful summer's day in August, 1981.
>
> As far as my conscious memory of it is concerned, I was simply in deep meditation. All of a sudden, I was inflamed. It was like a magnesium flare had gone off inside me. Brilliant white light—it was a little bit shocking. It was bright.
>
> The light was so strong that I could feel my eyes couldn't stand it, and that I was going to be struck blind like Paul was on the road to Damascus. It was just a shock, and I went into a different consciousness. It was unbelievable. The colors were intense, brilliant, you could feel the energy. You

could feel the vibratory energy of the different colors as separate. Here I am, without my glasses, and I'm nearsighted and I could see the pores in clover leaves thirty feet away. Plus a host of other things. That was an experience that opened me rather suddenly. I knew I was a different person when I came out of it, and I really didn't know who I was. It took a couple of years to know, like I still am learning. Other people have that occur with the same progression, but gradually. My wife says that the Lord has to hit some people with a two by four to get their attention. I think she's right.

I very definitely had the feeling that I had somehow made some connection with divinity. It seemed like I could hear things and see things, was conscious of things, that were out of this realm. It lasted a little time, I don't know how long. Long enough to have it do its work I guess.

I knew that I'd been touched by God. In that experience, I was one with God, and recognized that I had restructured my nature to be compatible with the spiritual change that had occurred in me. For instance, St. Paul, after he was struck on the road to Damascus, I think it took him seven years before he had everything sorted out and balanced, and was able to go out and teach. There's a restructuring of us that has to go on after such an experience. For me, it's still going on.

Finally, not all mystical experiences of Oneness need seem particularly spiritual or holy. Consider the following from SECOND WIND: THE MEMOIRS OF AN OPINIONATED MAN, the autobiography of Bill Russell, legendary center for the Boston Celtics and winner of seven consecutive National Basketball Association championships:

It was almost as if we were playing in slow motion. During those spells, I could almost sense . . . the next play. . . . I wanted to shout to my teammates "It's coming there!"–except that I knew everything would change if I did. My premonitions would be consistently correct and I always felt that that I not only knew all of the Celtics by heart but also all the opposing players and they all knew me.

Or consider Michael Jordan's description of his June 14, 1998 experience, on hitting the come-from-behind, game and title winning shot for what was to be the sixth NBA championship of his legendary career:

When I got that rebound, my thoughts were very positive. The crowd gets quiet. The moment starts to become the moment for me. That's part of Zen Buddhism–when you get in the moment, you know that you're there. Things start to move slowly. You start to see the court very well. You start reading what the defense is trying to do. And I saw that, I saw that moment. When I saw the moment of opportunity–to take advantage of it when [Bryon] Russell reached–I took advantage of that moment. I never doubted myself; I never doubted the whole game. . . . I knew that we would have an opportunity to win this game and I just wanted to be able to do that.

3. The Inner Voice and Oneness

Throughout history, certain persons have become famous as mystics. Who are such people?

The mystics have been perfectly normal people. They did not think of themselves as mystics, that was their language. It was natural to them–perfectly normal. They have been people like Jacob Boehm, a cobbler, pegging away at his shoes, who, looking up, saw in the geranium plant the reflection of the cosmos—the very soul of God; like Jesus looking into the heart of nature, like Moses reading God's law from a burning bush.

THE SCIENCE OF MIND, BY ERNEST HOLMES

The mystical experience of Oneness also touches the inner voice, and, at times the inner voice has a compelling component to it, which must be spoken out by the mystic.

Perhaps the most famous historic examples of Christian mystics were St. John of the Cross and Saint Theresa of Ávila, both sixteenth-century European mystics and close friends. There are extensive records of their experience of union with God, which include their experience with their inner voice. St. John of the Cross was highly suspect of "messages" received during states of union with the Divine. He set out to illuminate any possible delusion of mind that might create an experience of "messages." His ultimate advice was to throw out the "message," as too possibly suspect to be trusted, but to remember the "touch" or *toques* that comes to those who attain union with God.

Saint Theresa of Ávila, on the other hand, was less theologically trained than her friend, St. John of the Cross, and gave wider latitude to what she termed "locutions," which she defined as "words plainly formed, but which are not heard at all as if by the sense of hearing." Theresa of Ávila lived in the time of the Inquisition and was careful how she described her revelations. However, she was also bound by her vows of obedience to tell everything about her religious life to her assigned mentors. Hence, her story of her "locutions" is there, but guarded. Perhaps because of the Inquisition, she was the only Catholic mystic of her time who gave locutions, or speaking as God, credibility, with caution.

4. The Language of Oneness

We learn of Oneness through its many clues: synchronicity, coincidence, intuition. We can experience Oneness through the development of our contact with the inner voice. Pursuing the inner voice, the words we ultimately hear are those of Oneness. What are those words? Writers throughout history have given us examples of the unique language of Oneness. If you have never heard God speaking in the first person, it may be strange at first, but bear with us as it is explained. Here is an example from Robert Wall Crary's book, THE STILL SMALL VOICE:

I have told you that I Am God, that I Am you, and that you are me. Do you realize that I Am all of Life? Even more, are you aware that I Am all there is, that there is nothing but Me? I Am the Essence of everything that is known in your world, but more than that, of all the worlds you or anyone will ever know—the seen and the unseen. I Am All that exists in the entire Universe. How can that be? Listen and I will tell you.

I Am your own individualized Spiritual Self; and since I Am one in consciousness with God, I speak to you in the awareness that I Am God, even though I Am your personalized God Self within you. In this Oneness, I partake of God's Being in His Entirety. Hence, as I live in His Oneness and as I Am these things in Him, My Speaking is His Speaking through Me to you. Thus, I reveal to you His Nature, which is My Nature.

What does Mr. Crary mean? From what perspective is he writing these seemingly circular words? Is he saying that he is God? Is he writing down what he "hears" God saying, and, if so, why doesn't he just say, "I heard God say: 'I have told you that I Am God, that I Am you,'" and so forth?

What we are going to propose in this chapter is that we can elevate our consciousness to the point of Oneness with the Divine and speak from that point. When we do this, our language will have the first-person directness that Mr. Crary's writing has, which should, after all, be expected if we are in Oneness with All-That-Is, with the Divine.

This may sound startling, but it is nothing new. All of the great religious traditions make reference to this potential in humankind. For example,

Susan G. Shumsky, in her book, *DIVINE REVELATION*, analyzes the sayings of the historical Jesus as follows:

For example, Jesus stated:

"I AM the way, the truth and the life; no man cometh unto the Father, but by ME.

"I AM the light of the world: he that followeth ME shall not walk in darkness, but shall have the light of life.

"I AM the resurrection, and the life: he that believeth in ME, though he were dead, yet shall he live."

... Jesus was not alluding to his human embodiment or his ego identity when he said "I" or "ME." It is absurd to think that he was referring to his physical body when he stated, "Before Abraham was, I AM." He was speaking of God within him. He ... never claimed or desired to be deified.

Jesus said, "For I have not spoken of myself; but the Father which sent me, he gave me a commandment, what I should say, and what I should speak.

"Believest thou not that I AM in the Father and the Father in me? The words that I speak unto you I speak not of myself: but the Father that dwelleth in me, he doeth the works."

We submit that Jesus's statements referred to above, and Mr. Crary's statements quoted above, are coming from the same place–alignment in consciousness with Ultimate Reality. Any writing from that point of Oneness, that place of communion and unity, will necessarily reflect God's expressing His thoughts on the subject at hand, in unity with the human author aligned with that Oneness. Thus, "I AM the Light" written by a human author from the place of Oneness means simply that, viewed from God's perspective, He embodies Spirit luminosity, which infuses all of His creation.

This final expression of the inner voice is different from all that has preceded. It is a different quality: it is Oneness that speaks through the inner voice. At some point, human beings, at one with the inner voice, lift their consciousness up to the place of the I AM and are able to speak the inner voice as God, which is what occurs in the written example from Robert Wall Crary and in the New Testament speech of Jesus.

5. I AM THAT I AM

During one of his conversations with God, Moses asked God what to tell the people of Israel when they asked for God's name. God answered: "I AM THAT I AM." God also said, "this is My name forever" (Exodus 3:14).

Does this mean God's name is not "Richard" or "Jane" but "I AM THAT I AM"? I AM carries a certain quality that Richard and Jane do not. Richard and Jane are beings separate from myself. But, when I say I AM, I cannot help but also be included in the name. When I add I AM THAT, suddenly everything else in the universe is included. If that is God's name, it may be that God is All, including myself.

In working with the inner voice, there is a vibration that accompanies entering I AM consciousness. Lifting into that consciousness carries the frequency and power of God. When we reach the place of the I AM in our consciousness and speak from that place, we are speaking with the vibration and power of God.

How does a person elevate his or her consciousness into the I AM? This happens in meditative states when "I AM" (the personal "I") "THAT" (reaching upward) "I AM" (contacts God), which inherently results in the individual's recognizing that he or she is part of God, or Oneness.

Imagine the visual picture of an individual trying to contact God in a meditative state. The individual reaches upward, connects with and thereby inherently becomes God, or achieves Oneness ("I AM THAT I AM"). This experience, like falling in love, must be experienced to be fully understood, but the becoming Oneness equals "I AM THAT I AM," as was said in the Old Testament.

6. The Voice of Oneness in All Traditions

Mysticism is a vital element in Islam and describes the voice in union with God in the following way:

> There are seven chief attributes [to the Islamic mystic tradition]. One of those is the illumination of speech "mukallamun." The Word (kalam) comes to them sometimes audibly and from a certain direction, sometimes from no direction and

not through the ear, sometimes as an inner light having a definite shape; and in oneness with God they realize that all existent beings are their Word and that their words are without end.

> STUDIES IN ISLAMIC MYSTICISM,
> BY REYNOLD ALLEYNE NICHOLSON

The Sufi poet Hallaj expressed it in the following way:

> I am He whom I love, and he whom I love is I. We are two spirits dwelling in one body. If thou seest me, thou seest Him. And if thou seest Him, thou seest us both.

HALLAJ [FROM STUDIES IN ISLAMIC MYSTICISM]

The Hindu tradition, the oldest in history, in its ancient text, The Upanishads, states:

> I am That. Thou are That. All this is That. That alone is.

Because this expression is the ultimate reality, the realization of this truth brings about Brahman consciousness, or God consciousness.

> God is the real Self in me, I am That; He is the Self of all beings, I am That. All-pervading like the sky, I am That. Spotless pure consciousness, I am That.

> THE AVADHUTA GITA 1:6

Mystical experience and expressions of union with the Divine are also found in Judaism (in the Kabbalah), Taoism, Zen Buddhism and in all of the world's other great religions.

7. The Inner Voice, Oneness and the I AM Presence

> The inner voice is the distant, first heard cry of an approaching oneness with the I AM.

> ANONYMOUS

What is the "I AM"? Understood by different cultures in different ways, the "I AM" is the divine, nonmaterial spark that dwells in each of us and gives, to the unique being that each of us is, connection to and participation in God, and God in us. It signifies the manner in which "God created man in his own image" (*Genesis 1:27*). It is the eternal, perfect manifestation of divinity in a unique material being–you. Being part of God, the "I AM" in each of us is connected to every other part of God–it connects each of us to the Oneness. And it speaks to us through our own inner voice.

I AM is elegant in its simplicity. When we say I AM, we affirm that we exist, that we are conscious of our own existence and that our existence implies eternal inclusion of our unique being in God and eternal connection to the Oneness of all existence.

I AM is also the most fundamental sound. What is more fundamental to each of us than personal existence, the First Cause and our connection to It? Because sound is creative, I AM summons into existence, through the power of our connection with God, whatever follows the affirmation. "I AM rich" creates wealth; "I AM poor" creates lack. "I AM happy with the result" creates a good ending. "I AM really sick of this job" creates unhappy work.

Consider the following from Jack Hart:

I have the feeling sometimes that I am getting some wisdom that is not God's wisdom, but of some other being. It could be of a human being, it could be of a tree, it could be of an angelic kind of being, or some beings that we don't have words for, and that I'm touching it, in some way that I cannot express. But, it's not so much a oneness. There's a complete empathy that happens, and therefore there is an experience of oneness. But, it's almost like a holographic[6] experience, where I am a fragment, but within that fragment is experienced what I am one with. It doesn't feel like a merging, it feels like a–this magical dance of encompassing the whole, even while knowing that you're a part. That you are a part of the whole–the whole, of being a hologram. I feel that each of us is a hologram of infinity.

There seems to be a constant push, within me, that I can access at any time, for the experiencing of the "Am." No "I," no "That," just "Am." That life seems to be a verb. That all the forms that we see and we seem to

identify with are merely sort of points where the energy can flow between us, the energy flowing that's the existence. In a relationship, it's not the two people, it's the relationship that's real, and the two people just are a way that the relationship can be. Our bodies and different things are just ways that life can be. [My experience] for at least the last thirty years is just a constant feeling of moving from the "I am Jack" to "I am" to "am." Strangely, as the "I" is shed, it doesn't seem that the "I" is lost in some kind of wonderful abstract way, but just that "amness." The "I" is sort of needed for the "amness" in some way, but–so just the "amness" is what seems to me to be life, that life's a verb, it's not a subject, an object, it's a verb.

Why do we strive to listen to our inner voice, to understand the I AM and to access Oneness? Robert Wall Crary comments:

---

6   Currently created with laser technology, a hologram is an exact three-dimensional image of a three-dimensional object. Any part of a hologram exactly reproduces a fainter three-dimensional image of the entire original object.

If humanity could only come to recognize and fully accept the Presence of this Spirit within his very being, his own spiritual Counterpart, all of his lack, limitations, problems and suffering would gradually disappear from his consciousness and, hence, from the world.

So, keep following that yearning; it's worth the effort. Let your heart open to the experiences that lead you to the ultimate destination: union. Listen to the inner voice, for it is your faultless personal guide to Oneness with the Divine.

HOW TO

Oneness

TRY IT!

It has been said that there is no technique to experiencing Oneness, that all we can really do is to remove the blocks to it. Do you recall the feeling you had in an experience similar to any of the following instances?

- Focusing intently on another person with whom you shared unconditional love–a child or a spouse–and feeling the power of that moment.
- Feeling love in the area of your heart and consciously pushing that feeling of love outward toward nothing in particular–and feeling love coming back.
- Following the urge to speak out loud when in a contemplative state.
- Listening to a person chattering, and getting the feeling that the perfect thing for that person at that moment was for you to give them a touch on the arm or a consoling word.

TRY IT!

To experience the feeling of Oneness, you might try quieting your mind and selecting one of the following statements to focus on. Really try to concentrate on feeling the truth of the statement:

- "I AM" in perfect health.
- "I AM" the complete manifestation of my new home consistent with the good of the whole.
- "I AM" the perfect conclusion to this dispute.
- "I AM" a happy day, all day today.
- "I AM THAT I AM."

Where Does It Go From Here?

There is no death.
Only a change of worlds.

CHIEF SEATTLE

Look at me–I am poor and naked, but I
am the chief of the nation. We do not
want riches, but we do want to train our
children right. Riches would do us no
good. We could not take them with us to
the other world. We do not want riches.
We want peace and love.

CHIEF RED CLOUD

The journey may never be complete: following the inner voice may be an eternal quest. Where does it go from here? Here's where it has gone for the authors of this book.

Ellen:

In 1974 I was walking through a room and saw on a television news report this man half-turn toward what I recognized to be the Beverly Wilshire Hotel and smile at the camera. My inner voice strongly urged me at that moment to meet that man, although I didn't know why or how. It was apparently the first trip for this man to the United States from his native country; he was known as the Dalai Lama. I was drawn by my inner voice to meet this foreign dignitary; that's about as much as I knew about him at that time. Never before or since have I run off to meet somebody that I saw on television, but I got the most strong inner voice urging that I've

ever had to go find that man. I knew that he was at that hotel and I decided that I was going to go meet him there. I went there and found a Tibetan that looked like a monk standing outside of a hotel suite with a little table with a bowl of fruit and some flowers on it. He told me that the Lama was out on another appointment and that he wouldn't be back for a while. I said I'd wait. He interviewed me for several hours. We talked and he asked me at length about my spiritual life and my training, whether I had worked with a teacher or not. We had lots of good laughs—he had that wonderful Tibetan chuckle—but we also had some very serious conversation about my spiritual life (which had had virtually nothing to do with Buddhism). Then the elevator doors opened and the Dalai Lama stepped out with an entourage—the whole elevator was full of people. The monk that I had been talking to at the door walked up to the Dalai Lama and spoke to him; they were whispering back and forth. His Holiness then told all the people behind him to wait and walked with me and the monk into the hotel suite, leaving the door open.

He asked me: "Do you have any questions?" and smiled at me with that smile I had seen on the television news report. I said: "No." I didn't really have any questions, and I actually didn't know what I was doing there. He put his hands out and I just put my hands in his. Then it was as if we existed only from the waist up. There was an egg of light surrounding us, and the egg started to rise. It was like an oval of light and it started to lift up. It's very hard to put an experience like this into words, but very soon all there was was light. We stayed in that state for what seemed like a long time—I thought the whole thing took about twenty minutes, but it might have been a much shorter time, because you lose track of time in a situation like that. Then he smiled and I said goodbye and

walked out. As I was leaving and walking toward the elevator, an old Hopi elder, a short man with totally white hair and a headband around his head, was coming to meet the Lama. The Lama was standing in the hallway—so the three of us were standing there sort of looking at each other—and I just felt like this was the most significant moment—I had no idea what its significance was—but it really felt like a powerful moment with the three of us there.

I think that this experience had a profound effect on my life. When I left the room, the window at the end of the hotel hallway was just ablaze with the colors of a beautiful sunset—there was all yellow and pink outside. I don't know if it was my state of mind or the actual colors, but it was a very beautiful moment. I had the sense that this event was going to go into my future, and this was going to affect my life. I didn't really know what the effect was at that time, but—I look back and that was twenty-five years ago–I left there with a sense of inner purpose, not one that I could articulate, but that I was clearly set on a road now. I clearly had a direction. It had to do with service; that's all I could say; I was really ready to give from that day on.

Jim:

In 1992 I was a practicing international commercial litigator and a relatively new member of the American Bar Association's International Section. At that time, some of my friends interested in international cooperation suggested that I go with them to attend the United Nations Conference on Ecology and Development (the "Earth Summit") in Rio de Janeiro. I had never before attended a large international conference; I was busy at work; and it didn't strike me as much of a vacation or likely to be otherwise productive.

A few weeks passed and I received a newsletter from the American Bar Association noting that, as a nongovernmental organization with observer status at the Earth Summit, it was entitled to appoint two representatives to attend the governmental sessions of the conference. When I saw the piece, I immediately got the inner urging to call the ABA's headquarters in Chicago and ask about being appointed a representative. I remember telephoning a pleasant person at ABA headquarters and asking how to proceed. She first advised that there were many, many people ahead of me with better credentials and experience, and only two slots, but she gave me the name of an ABA official who would be participating in making the final decision. Coincidentally, I had actually shaken hands with this individual once before. I called him and asked to be considered, but he was noncommittal. About a half an hour later, I received a call from the pleasant person I had first contacted at ABA headquarters. With shock in her voice, she advised that I would indeed be one of the two selected.

The rest of the event went that way—one serendipitous, exciting, fascinating, life-changing person, place or thing after the next. On the final day of the Earth Summit, sixty seats in the Plenary Hall were reserved for official representatives from the participating non-governmental organizations. Of the thousands of eligible representatives, only sixty could attend. I got ready to go even before the selections were announced: I somehow knew I'd be there.

I was selected (one of only nine from North America's 360 participating nongovernmental organizations) and it was an incredible experience. In one day, in one meeting hall, the leaders of more than 50 percent of the world's population each personally delivered a similar message about a global problem: as eloquently and succinctly put that day by Fidel Castro, we were in danger of losing an important species through loss of habitat:

man. The speakers included Prime Minister P. V. Narasimha Rao of India, Li Peng of China, Helmut Kohl of Germany, England's John Major, Brian Mulroney of Canada, Prince Rainier of Monaco, Fidel Castro, and the presidents of Portugal, Turkey, Argentina, Brazil, Morocco and many other countries. George Bush spoke later in the day, and the Dalai Lama spoke earlier in another Rio venue. Looking back on it, I realize that I learned from the event that there was more going on in life than international commercial litigation and that I wanted to be part of the solution to the world's problems, and not part of the problem, a decision that had been made by the many capable leaders I heard speak that day. I probably never would have come to that realization unless I had listened to my inner voice's urging to get in touch with that first ABA official, and this book would probably never have been written.

Grateful acknowledgement is made for permission to reprint the following material: